TABLE OF CONTENTS

ACRONYMS

9/11	11 September 2001
AOR	Area of Responsibility
COCOM	Combatant Command
DoD	Department of Defense
DoS	Department of State
GRP	Government of the Republic of the Philippines
MARFORPAC	Marine Forces Pacific
NMS	National Military Strategy
NSS	National Security Strategy
PACAF	Pacific Air Forces
PACFLT	Pacific Fleet
QDR	Quadrennial Defense Review
SOCPAC	Special Operations Command - Pacific
SOF	Special Operations Forces
USARPAC	United States Army Pacific
USPACOM	United States Pacific Command
USSOCOM	United States Special Operations Command

ILLUSTRATIONS

TABLES

Page

.

CHAPTER 1

INTRODUCTION

On 25 April 1898, the United States formally declared war on Spain. Six days

later on 1 May 1898, Commodore George Dewey of the United States uttered the words,

"You may fire when you are ready, Gridley." Following that phrase, the United States

Asiatic Squadron from Hong Kong defeated Admiral Patricio Montojo y Pasaron's

Spanish Squadron in Manila Bay of the Philippine Islands.[1] This event began the United

States' interaction and influence in the Philippines.

For the next four years, while working multiple treaties with Europeans, the

United States fought a Philippine insurgency across the Philippine islands. By July 1902,

when the war ended, more than 4,200 U.S. soldiers, 20,000 Filipino insurgents/soldiers,

and 200,000 civilians were dead.[2] The United States maintained sovereignty over the

Philippine Islands for another 44 years until 1946.

On 4 July 1946, under the guidance of the United Nations, the United States and

Philippines signed the Treaty of Manila. Article 1 of the treaty established the Philippines

as its own nation. "The United States of America agrees to withdraw and surrender, and

does hereby withdraw and surrender, all right of possession, supervision, jurisdiction,

control or sovereignty existing and exercised by the United States of America in and over

---

[1]Hispanic Division, Library of Congress, "Chronology for the Philippine Islands and Guam in the Spanish-American War," World of 1898, http://www.loc.gov/rr/ hispanic/1898/chronphil.html (accessed 7 May 2012).

[2]Ibid.

1

the territory and the people of the Philippine Islands."[3] Even though the United States

was relinquishing control over the Philippines, they did not completely leave the new

nation of the Philippines. In fact, Article 1 of the Treaty of Manila covered additional

United States military presence and possession of bases in the Philippines. The treaty

stated, "the use of such bases, necessary appurtenances to such bases, and the rights

incident thereto, as the United States of America, by agreement with the Republic of the

Philippines, may deem necessary to retain for the mutual protection of the United States

of America and of the Republic of the Philippines."[4] This language in the treaty afforded

the United States a strategic partner in the Pacific with operating air and naval military

installations until 1991. For the new Filipino nation, the treaty allowed the United States

to protect the Philippines from attack.

In 1991, the United States closed its two military bases in the Philippines. Clark

Air Force Base and Subic Bay Naval Base were major contributors to Pacific stability.

The United States had been leasing the land for these two bases from the Government of

the Republic of the Philippines. Mount Pinatubo erupted on 15 June 1991, damaging the

United States' base at Clark Air Field.[5] Later that year, the Philippine Government chose

---

[3]United States of America and Philippines, *Treaty of Manila* (New York: United Nations, 1946).

[4]Ibid.

[5]Matt Rosenburg, "Mount Pinatubo Eruption," About.com, http://geography. about.com/od/globalproblemsandissues/a/pinatubo.htm (accessed 12 May 2012).

not to renew the leases of Clark and Subic Bay. This decision caused the American military to leave the Philippine islands.[6]

In the twenty-one years since the United States left their permanent bases in the Philippine Islands, the United States military and government responded every time the Filipino people have needed them. These events can be natural disasters like mudslides or the annual "shoulder-to-shoulder" Balikatan exercise.[7] It has been 114 years since Commodore Dewey defeated the Spanish in Manila Bay. Collaboration has defined the United States-Philippine relationship since Philippine independence in 1946.

Today, American and Filipino cooperation is important to both nations. There are an estimated 300,000 Americans living in the Philippines and over 600,000 Americans visit the Philippines each year.[8] There are over two million Americans of Filipino descent living in America.[9] In 2001, President George W. Bush and President Gloria Macapagal-Arroyo noted that the American-Filipino "alliance remains a pillar of the U.S. security presence in Asia, which helps preserve a strategic balance that favors freedom and

---

[6]Martin W. Lewis, "The Legacy of U.S. Military Bases in the Philippines," GeoCurrents, http://geocurrents.info/geopolitics/the-legacy-of-u-s-military-bases-in-the-philippines (accessed 12 May 2012).

[7]John Pike, "Exercise Balikatan 'Shouldering the Load Together,'" GlobalSecurity.org, http://www.globalsecurity.org/military/ops/balikatan.htm (accessed 12 May 2012).

[8]U.S. Department of State, "Philippines," Bureau of East Asian and Pacific Affairs, http://www.state.gov/r/pa/ei/bgn/2794.htm#relations (accessed 21 September 2012).

[9]White House, "U.S.-Philippine Joint Statement on Defense Alliance," http://georgewbush-whitehouse.archives.gov/news/releases/2001/11/20011120-14.html (accessed 21 September 2012).

promotes prosperity throughout the region."[10] They further agreed that terrorist activities

across the globe, to include activities in the Philippines, require a strong defense

partnership for the coming years. Both leaders believe that the best way to accomplish

this partnership is through "increased training, exercises and other joint activities."[11]

American presence in the Philippines is important to both nations as evidenced by

multiple statements from leaders of both nations. Consideration of the cultural

sensitivities of permanent American forces in the Philippines is imperative in achieving

the defensive partnership between the two nations. Counterterrorism operations in the

southern Philippines and naval support for maritime trade are paramount in boosting this

relationship.

The events of 9/11 further enhanced the link between the United States and the

Philippines. After America appealed for global assistance following the attacks of 9/11,

Philippine President Arroyo announced that the GRP would go "all out" to provide

assistance and to implement U.N. Security Council Resolution 1368. She offered Filipino

airspace and seaports to the American military.[12] The GRP opened the country to

American support in finding terrorists within the Philippines Islands.

Following multiple references to a global strategy change, President Barack

Obama released new strategic planning guidance for the Department of Defense (DoD) in

January 2012. This guidance set out to transition the DoD from focusing on the Middle

---

[10]Ibid.

[11]Ibid.

[12]Colonel Romulo Supapo, *U.S.-Philippines Security Relations: Its Implications for the Global War on Terrorism* (Carlisle Barracks, PA: U.S. Army War College, 2004), 11.

East to move to a Pacific focus.[13] Many people have coined this transition as the "pivot to the Pacific." What will this shift mean for the Philippines? The United States' renewed interest in the Pacific begs the question as to what is the right composition of forces to execute this new strategy. In the Philippines, should the forces that are best suited for a strategic impact in the Philippine Islands be United States' conventional or special operations forces?

---

[13]White House, "Sustaining U.S. Global Leadership: Priorities for 21st Century Defense," January 2012.

Figure 1.   The Philippine Islands

Source: Department of State, "Philippines," http://www.state.gov/p/eap/ci/rp/ (accessed 24 October 2012).

The military forces that currently reside in the Pacific area of responsibility (AOR) fall under the geographic combatant command (COCOM) authority of United States Pacific Command (USPACOM). Pacific Fleet (PACFLT) presents USPACOM naval forces. United States Army Pacific (USARPAC) presents USPACOM ground forces. Marine Forces Pacific (MARFORPAC) presents USPACOM marine forces. Pacific Air Forces (PACAF) presents USPACOM air power. Finally, Special Operations Command – Pacific (SOCPAC) presents USPACOM's special operations forces.[14] These forces meet the strategic goals of the United States in the Pacific, which includes thirty-six countries in the USPACOM area of responsibility.

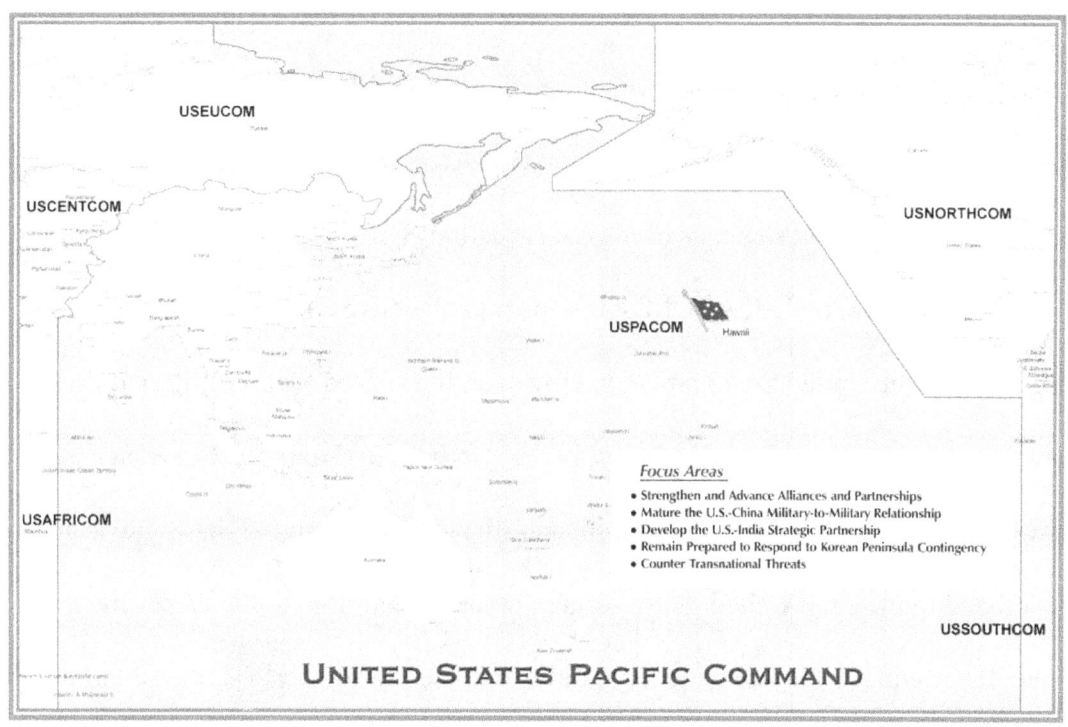

Figure 2.   USPACOM AOR

Source: USPACOM Website, http://www.pacom.mil (accessed 12 May 2012).

---

[14]USPACOM, "United States Pacific Command," http://www.pacom.mil (accessed 12 May 2012).

USPACOM's stated mission is that it "protects and defends, in concert with other U.S. government agencies, the territory of the United States, its people, and its interests. With allies and partners, the U.S. Pacific Command is committed to enhancing stability in the Asia-Pacific region by promoting security cooperation, encouraging peaceful development, responding to contingencies, deterring aggression, and when necessary, fighting to win."[15] In order to meet this mission, USPACOM deploys its functional component commands across the above AOR with seven objectives: (1) Protect the homeland; (2) Maintain a robust military capability; (3) Develop cooperative security arrangements; (4)Strengthen and expand relationships with allies and partners; (5) Reduce susceptibility to violent extremism; (6) Deter military aggression; and (7) Deter adversaries from using weapons of mass destruction[16]

Understanding USPACOM's mission and objectives in the Pacific region is necessary to the United States strategy. However, the United States military does not have the deciding vote. In each country in the Pacific, the Department of State is the controlling mechanism for all American activities under the United States government positioned to meet the United States foreign policy. According to the Department of State, the "central U.S. foreign policy goal is that the Philippines becomes a more stable, prosperous and well-governed nation that is no longer a safe haven for terrorists."[17] This foreign policy goal became the Department of State strategic vision. The Mission to the

---

[15]Ibid.

[16]Ibid.

[17]U.S. Mission to the Philippines, *Country Assistance Strategy Philippines: 2009-2013* (Washington, DC: Department of State, 2009), 2.

Philippines states this vision as, "a more prosperous, well-governed and stable democracy that is able to meet the needs of its people, especially the poor."[18] The question now is how the United States prioritizes efforts in the Philippines.

In the Philippines, the Department of State has four clearly stated objectives. These objectives are: "accelerating growth through improved competitiveness; strengthening governance, rule of law, and the fight against corruption; investing in people to reduce poverty; and promoting a peaceful and secure Philippines."[19] The purpose of this paper will be to determine what type of force, conventional forces or special operations forces are best suited to support these four strategic goals in the Philippines.

Analysis of some governing documents that affect Philippine engagement will help discern the priority of forces to support the above stated objectives. Such documents as the *National Security Strategy*, *Joint Vision 2020*, *USPACOM Strategic Guidance*, and others will lead to needs in the Republic of the Philippines. After the needs have been identified, the forces required need to be assessed. Comparing the USPACOM forces as to which are best positioned, most flexible and are the most regionally focused answers what type of forces provide strategic impact in support of the Department of State goals.

<u>Assumptions</u>

A major assumption of this thesis is that special operations forces from all services assigned to the Pacific will be sufficient to meet the United States objectives in

---

[18]Ibid., 3.

[19]Ibid., 4, 5.

the Philippines. Extrapolating information from the governing documents and comparing that information against the four objectives is a method to alleviate this assumption. In order to find common ground to determine the right type of force, the assumption is that connecting the governing documents is enough to establish a link to align either conventional forces or special operations forces in order to meet the goals in the Philippines. The final assumption is that the United States will continue to devote national resources in light of current fiscal environments to support the Filipino people as it has done for one hundred and fourteen years.

Definitions

Conventional forces: "Those forces other than designated special operations forces."[20]

Effect: "A change to a condition, behavior, or degree of freedom."[21]

Special operations: "Operations requiring unique modes of employment, tactical techniques, equipment and training often conducted in hostile, denied, or politically sensitive environments and characterized by one or more of the following: time sensitive, clandestine, low visibility, conducted with and/or through indigenous forces, requiring regional expertise, and/or a high degree of risk."[22]

---

[20]Joint Chiefs of Staff, Joint Publication (JP) 1-02, *Department of Defense Dictionary of Military and Associated Terms* (Washington, DC: Government Printing Office, November 2010 (as amended through January 2012)), 73.

[21]Ibid., 105.

[22]Ibid., 310.

Special operations forces: "Those Active and Reserve Component forces of the

Military Services designated by the Secretary of Defense and specifically organized,

trained, and equipped to conduct and support special operations."[23]

Strategic: Far reaching efforts designed to have a lasting impact at a national level

Scope

The overall goal is to determine what type of force best supports the United

States' four strategic goals in the Philippines. Although there are other opinions on what

the United States' focus should be in the Philippines, the 2009-2013 goals of the United

States Department of State[24] are the litmus test for United States military involvement in

the Philippines in the future. This effort will not analyze counter-Chinese expansion

theories or recommended numbers of forces required to meet United States objectives.

The conclusions will not make base relocation recommendations or imply that the United

States needs to reestablish permanent bases in the Philippines. As stated earlier, the

Filipino people have indicated that they do not want permanent United States bases on

Filipino soil at this time.

Limitations

Due to the sensitivity of operations, any reference to current operations in the

Philippines will remain unclassified and information about current operations comes from

open sources. Because it is impossible to ascertain the precise requirements of the future

engagements, information from governing documents focus a concept of future

---

[23]Ibid.

[24]U.S. Mission to the Philippines, Appendix B.

requirements in the Philippines. Filipino and American strategic interaction projections from the United States Department of State provide the baseline for strategic goals. Despite multiple attempts to gain supporting documents from USPACOM and Joint Chiefs, additional insights into current American military strategies in regards to the Philippines were unattainable.

Delimitations

Research into the China's impact on Filipino people is beyond the scope of this paper. This includes issues of state sovereignty in the South China Sea, which are very important to the Government of the Philippines. At the 30 April 2012 "2+2" meeting between the United States and the Philippines, United States Secretary of State Clinton addressed the sovereignty issue. She stated, "While we do not take sides on the competing sovereignty claims to land features in the South China Sea, as a Pacific power we have a national interest in freedom of navigation, the maintenance of peace and stability, respect for international law, and the unimpeded, lawful commerce across our sea lanes."[25] The Straits of Malacca are important to trade and influence the four strategic goals, but are an issue beyond the scope of this paper. These issues can shape future strategic goals of the United States in the Philippines; however, they could stand as research papers on their own.

---

[25]Hillary Rodham Clinton, Remarks With Secretary of Defense Leon Panetta, Philippines Foreign Secretary Albert del Rosario, and Philippines Defense Secretary Voltaire Gazmin After Their Meeting, Washington, DC, 30 April 2012.

Importance

With a renewed focus on the Pacific, called the "pivot to the Pacific," and United States military forces returning from major operations in Southwest Asia, proper force application in the region will affect future Pacific engagements.[26] The size of the USPACOM AOR calls for a judicious use and stationing of the forces required to meet the intent of the USPACOM engagement strategy. Secretary of Defense Leon Panetta spoke to the importance of the Philippines as a strategic partner in the Pacific at the "2+2" meeting in April 2012. He stated, "We are enhancing our defense cooperation and expanding security partnerships throughout the region in order to sustain peace and stability, and we are committed to continuing our robust, stabilizing presence in that region."[27] Based on statements by the President, the Secretary of State and the Secretary of Defense this year, America is reaffirming its support to the Pacific and in particular the support to the Filipino people at the request of GRP. The conclusions will address what type of forces should carry the load to meet the United States strategic goals in the Philippines.

Figures

Figure 1 is a map of the Philippines from the United States Department of State website, which shows the island structure of the nation.[28] Figure 2 is a map of the

---

[26]Congressional Research Service, *Pivot to the Pacific? The Obama Administration's "Rebalancing" Toward Asia* (Washington, DC: Congressional Research Service, 2012), 1.

[27]Ibid.

[28]Department of State, "Philippines," http://www.state.gov/p/eap/ci/rp/ (accessed 13 May 2012).

13

USPACOM area of responsibility from the USPACOM website.[29] This map is important to show the location of the Philippines in the vast USPACOM area of responsibility.

Tables

Table 1 represents how the analysis conclusions are determined. Table 2 displays the current United States' armed forces in the Pacific. Table 3 comes from the United States Department of State Country Assistance Strategy for the Philippines 2009-2013.[30] Appendix B of the document addresses the four priority goals for the United States in the Philippines. These goals will be the baseline comparison for military requirements in the Philippines. Table 4 shows the comparison rubric. Table 5 shows the additional factors rubric. Table 6 shows the results of comparing the goals in table 3 against the USPACOM functional component commands. Table 7 shows the results of comparing the USPACOM functional component commands against the rubric in table 5. Table 8 shows the analysis conclusions.

This Introduction provides a brief history and a baseline understanding as to what types of forces are best to support United States' goals in the Philippines. The following Literature Review describes the sources used in the analysis of this paper.

---

[29]USPACOM.

[30]U.S. Mission to the Philippines, Appendix B.

14

CHAPTER 2

LITERATURE REVIEW

The introduction focused on the historical significance of United States-Philippines relationship though a short glimpse at the national relationships. This historical baseline has led to the current collaboration between the two nations. What follows describes the type of sources used to analyze the type of force required. In order to determine the right type of military force to support the United States' strategic goals in the Philippines, the focus is on the current United States Department of State objectives. The objectives are "accelerating growth through improved competitiveness; strengthening governance, rule of law, and the fight against corruption; investing in people to reduce poverty; and promoting a peaceful and secure Philippines."[31]

Source documents provide the reference data needed to determine the recommended type of force needed to support the above stated strategic goals. The source information divisions include historical support documents concerning early relationships between the United States and the Philippines, United States' guidelines and political statements, United States' governing documents, Filipino sources, and any uncategorized sources used as reference material.

Historical Support

In order to determine the recommended forces to support United States' national objectives in the Philippines, it is important to understand the historical relationship between the two nations. The main source used to trace the connected history of the

_____

[31]Ibid.

United States is Library of Congress website. The Hispanic Division of the Library of Congress created a "Chronology for the Philippine Islands and Guam in the Spanish-American War."[32] This source provides insight into the official first efforts by the United States at securing the Philippine Islands and the chronology of the United States' efforts in the Philippine region. The early history of the United States in the Philippines encompassed an insurgent and brutal war with the Filipino people that still resonate in the mind of some Filipinos today. The Hispanic Division at the Library of Congress timeline provides a useful transition in the history from the late 1800s and early 1900s until the Treaty of Manila in 1946. This includes American military support to the Filipinos during the World Wars.

The Treaty of Manila paved the way for the current United States and Philippines relationship. Ushered by the United Nations, this treaty affirmed the independent nation of the Philippines without the United States as a Filipino nation overseer. The first article of the treaty afforded the United States an ability to have military bases in the Philippines in order to provide outward security to the young nation following the invasions of the World Wars.[33] Because the Philippines remain a sovereign nation, the host nation can determine how long the United States could hold permanent military bases in the island nation.

Mr. Martin Lewis' "The Legacy of U.S. Military Bases in the Philippines," provides the insight into the end of United States' permanent basing in the Philippines.[34]

---

[32]Hispanic Division.

[33]United States of America and Philippines.

[34]Lewis.

16

This historical source provides insight to the shaping of today's relationship between the United States and the Philippines as it describes why the United States' military bases, designed to protect the Filipinos from outside threats, in the Philippines closed. With the closing of Clark Air Force Base and Subic Bay in 1991, the interaction and mutual defense of the United States and the Philippines took a less permanent footing and leads to the current supportive relationship.

United States Current Guidelines and Political Statements

The baseline comparison information for this paper comes from the United States Department of State, *Country Assistance Strategy for the Philippines from 2009-2013*. This document's Appendix B provides the four priority goals for the United States' interaction in the Philippines. These goals are not in priority order. Matching conventional and special operations forces against the four goals of "accelerating growth through improved competitiveness; strengthening governance, rule of law, and the fight against corruption; investing in people to reduce poverty; and promoting a peaceful and secure Philippines" are the basis of chapter 4.[35] This strategy falls in line with execution and consistent statements to support the Philippines by United States national leadership. Even though not all of these goals directly require military support, the United States military activities in the Philippines are just one national instrument of power available to achieve these goals.

United States Chairman of the Joint Chiefs of Staff General Dempsey serves as the lead military initiator of United States strategic goals. When asked by Carnegie's

---

[35]U.S. Mission to the Philippines, Appendix B.

Jessica Mathews on 1 May 2012, where the United States stands with the Philippines and China he stated, "We're bouncing ourselves back into the Pacific. That's not a containment strategy for China."[36] The Chairmen's statements in the Mathew's interview demonstrate that the United States finds many countries, to include the Philippines, are important for national strategy.

The United States' Secretary of State Hillary Clinton is a very vocal supporter of the American interaction with the Philippines. In November 2011, while addressing the Asia-Pacific Economic Cooperation in Hawai'i, she spoke of the importance of the Pacific region to the United States Secretary Clinton stated the United States' "commitment to democracy and human rights is shared by many nations in the region, in particular our treaty allies—Japan, South Korea, Australia, the Philippines, and Thailand."[37] In April 2012, Secretary Clinton and United Secretary of Defense attended the first-ever "2+2" meeting with their Filipino counterparts. She continued her support of the United States' commitment to the Philippines by her description of the purpose of the meeting. Secretary Clinton stated, "With the growing security and economic importance of the Asia Pacific, the United States is actively working to strengthen our alliances, build new partnerships, and engage more systematically in the region's multilateral institutions."[38] The United States continued interaction with the GRP is critical to maintaining Pacific-wide security. Following the "2+2" meeting, the United

---

[36]Jessica Tuchman Mathews, *A Conversations with General Martin Dempsey* (Washington, DC: Carnegie Endowment for International Peace, 2012), 15.

[37]Clinton, "America's Pacific Century" (Honolulu, HI, 2011).

[38]Clinton, Remarks with Secretary of Defense.

States' Secretary of Defense, Leon Panetta, stressed the continued importance of interaction between the two nations. He addressed General Dempsey's "bounce to the Pacific."[39]

> The new U.S. defense strategy that we rolled out earlier this year recognized that one of the important regions of the world that we must focus on and that America's future security depends on is the Asia Pacific region. As a resident Pacific power, the United States is committed to a rule-based regional order that promotes viable and vibrant trade and the freedom of navigation. We are enhancing our defense cooperation and expanding security partnerships throughout the region in order to sustain peace and stability, and we are committed to continuing our robust, stabilizing presence in that region.[40]

The Secretary of Defense's statement helps to focus the efforts of USPACOM's efforts in the Philippines. These statements align with the four United States' goals in the Philippines. National leadership consistency when dealing with the GRP and United States military efforts in the region is critical towards overall accomplishment of the national strategic goals.

<u>United States Governing Documents</u>

Linking current political guidelines to governing documents is the key to discerning the proper type of force to support United States' strategic objectives in the Philippines. The main governing documents for analysis include the United States' *National Security Strategy*,[41] the *National Military Strategy*,[42] the Chairman of the Joint

---

[39]Mathews.

[40]Clinton, Remarks with Secretary of Defense.

[41]White House, *National Security Strategy* (Washington, DC: Government Printing Office, 2010).

[42]Department of Defense, *National Military Strategy* (Washington, DC: Government Printing Office, 2011).

Chiefs of Staff's (CJCS) *Joint Vision 2020*,[43] and the *USPACOM Strategic Guidance*.[44] These documents provide the baseline for how the United States uses its forces in the Pacific region.

Taking these documents at face value and comparing them to the current political commentary leads to the information needed to begin considerations of United States' military force structure required to support the Department of State goals. Comparing the USPACOM forces as to which are best positioned, most flexible and are the most regionally focused answers what type of forces provide strategic impact in support of the Department of State goals. The important goal is to provide a recommendation of what type of force, conventional or special, to use in order to meet Pacific strategic ends. Vandenbroucke lamented that "U.S. decision makers should be especially vigilant to ensure that strategic special operations are used only as they should be used; as truly operations of the last resort."[45] These words are critical for consideration if this paper determines that special operations forces are the preferred force to support the four Department of State strategic goals in the Philippines.

Filipino Sources

It would be difficult to determine the best military force to support the United States strategic goals in the Philippines without considering the Filipino perspective. On

---

[43] Joint Chiefs of Staff, *Joint Vision 2020* (Washington, DC: Government Printing Office, June 2000).

[44] ADM Robert F. Willard, *United States Pacific Strategic Guidance* (Honolulu, HI: USPACOM, 2011).

[45] Lucien S. Vandenbroucke, *Perilous Options: Special Operations as an Instrument of U.S. Foreign Policy* (New York: Oxford University Press, 1993), 181.

30 April 2012, the senior leaders of the United States Department of State and Department of Defense met with Philippines' Foreign Secretary and Defense Secretary met for a first-ever "2+2" meeting. The focus of the meeting was to ensure that the United States and the Philippines remain on the same page as the two countries move forward into the future. Filipino Defense Secretary Albert del Rosario stated that the meeting

> reaffirmed our shared obligations under our mutual defense treaty and underscored the necessity of ensuring that our alliance remains robust, agile, and responsive. We committed to jointly explore modalities by which the President could build a minimum credible defense posture and agreed to prioritize high-value and high-impact joint military exercises and training to meet our common objectives.[46]

The insight from Secretary Clinton's Filipino counterpart supports understanding the parallel between the United States' goals and the host nation goals. Secretary Voltaire Gazmin stated that the meeting was a "manifestation of the mutual desire of the Philippines and the U.S. to further deepen our strategic partnership. After watching our alliance endure through the years, we deem it crucial to prepare for the security challenges of today and tomorrow."[47]

In order to prepare for future challenges, the Government of the Republic of the Philippines (GRP) issued their *Department of National Defense Planning Guidance for 2013-2018*. This document "provides direction for conducting the 2013-2018 program and 2018 budget development process."[48] Chapter 2 of this document addresses the

---

[46]Clinton, Remarks with Secretary of Defense.

[47]Ibid.

[48]Department of National Defense, *Defense Planning Guidance 2013-2018* (Manila, Philippines: Department of National Defense, 2012), 2.

21

national security concerns from the Filipino perspective. The Filipino government feels that their core security concerns are territorial defense, maritime security, natural disasters, internal security, and peripheral security concerns like good governance.[49] The *National Defense Planning Guidance* concerns directly tie to the United States Department of State priority goals of strengthening governance and promoting a peaceful and secure Philippines.[50] The aligning of goals by both countries is paramount to success in the Pacific.

The government of the Philippines furthers its intent with its strategic military interactions with USPACOM, particularly through the Mutual Defense Board/Security Engagement Board. The Executive Committee for these two boards met from 7-10 May 2012 to discuss contingency plans, information sharing, AFP upgrades, Maritime Security, US Regional Initiatives and the Ulugan Bay Development.[51] There will be a follow-on meeting in November 2012 to finalize AFP-US Military events for 2013. At these board meetings, the military leadership is able to effect the military interactions for both special operations and conventional forces in the Philippines. The United States can assure that it puts the right forces to the front in order to meet the overall United States strategic goals in the Philippines.

---

[49]Ibid., 5-7.

[50]U.S. Mission to the Philippines, Appendix B.

[51]Maj Gen Michael A. Keltz, and MGEN Roy O. Deveraturda, "Executive Committee Republic of the Philippines–United States of America Mutual Defense Board/Security Engagement Board (Camp Smith MCBH, HI: USPACOM, 2012).

Additional Perspectives

Besides American military and governmental insights, as well as Filipino insights, it is important to look at different perspectives on American involvement in the Philippines. Sheldon Simon presents that other nations besides the United States have a vested interest in the Philippines. Mr. Simon states that Australia "has developed bilateral security dialogues" with the Philippines to include signing a counterterrorism memorandum between the two nations in the past year.[52] Japan even provided aid packages to the Filipino people in Mindanao.[53] Close support from other Pacific partner nations provides additional resources to the Filipino people. Assuring that American efforts do not duplicate efforts between the Philippines and nations like Australia and Japan are important. Americans must be aware that other nations have interests in the Philippines.

Miscellaneous Sources

Additionally, other sources that do not fit into the above categories of historical, United States current guidelines and political statements, United States governing documents, or Filipino sources provide additional support to this paper. These documents include Joint Publications, like Joint Publication 1-02, that explains the terms used.[54] Furthermore, during the analysis of the type of forces needed to support the four strategic

---

[52]Sheldon Simon, "The United States, Japan, and Australia: Security Linkages to Southeast Asia" (The New Security Environment—Implications For American Security Conference, 4-5 April 2011, The National Defense University, Washington, DC), 6.

[53]Ibid., 7.

[54]Joint Chiefs of Staff, JP 1-02.

goals, aligning defined special operations capabilities from Joint Publication 3-05 is critical to the overall conclusion.[55] Sources like Lucien Vanderbroucke's *Perilous Options* provide analysis of the use of special operations at the strategic level as an instrument of national power.[56]

Additionally, using new agreements signed between the United States and the Philippines provide insight into the future interactions between the two countries. On 16 November 2011, aboard the *USS Fitzgerald* in Manila Bay, Secretary Clinton and Secretary Rosario signed the Manila Declaration.[57] According to the text of this new treaty, the two nations will continue to support each other in mutual defense situations in order to combat threats.

> We are determined to continue our bilateral cooperation in addressing broader regional and global challenges, including maritime security and threats to security such as climate change, nuclear proliferation, terrorism, and transnational crime. We are committed to continuing our close and effective cooperation to counter al-Qaida-linked terrorist groups in the southern Philippines.[58]

New treaties and agreements like the *Manila Treaty* will continue to shape the relationship between the two nations. Furthermore, they will shape how the United States achieves its strategic goals in the Philippines.

Another source comes from the United States Congressional Research in the report "The Republic of the Philippines and U.S. Interests." The insight from this

---

[55]Joint Chiefs of Staff, Joint Publication (JP) 3-05, *Special Operations* (Washington, DC: Government Printing Office, 2011).

[56]Vandenbroucke.

[57]United States of America, Government of Republic of the Philippines, *Manila Declaration* (Manila, Philippines, 2011).

[58]Ibid.

document analyzes the security ties, military relations, counterterrorism cooperation and other connections between the United States and the Philippines.[59]

Multiple types of sources shape the analysis to discern the right type of military force, conventional or special operations, to achieve the Unites States four strategic objectives in the Philippines. Dividing these sources into historical support documents, United States' current guidelines and political statements, United States' governing documents, Filipino sources, and any miscellaneous sources of significance groups the sources along common themes or approaches.

The next chapter of this paper defines the methodology needed to conduct the analysis to determine the right type of force to support the four United States' objectives in the Philippines. After the methodology explanation, the sources defined in this chapter help determine the answer to the thesis.

---

[59]Thomas Lum, *The Republic of the Philippines and the U.S. Interests* (Washington, DC: Congressional Research Service, 2012), 6-7.

CHAPTER 3

RESEARCH METHODOLOGY

The last chapter focused on the types of sources used in this thesis in order to determine the right type of forces to support the United States' strategic goals in the Philippines. This chapter explains how the analysis of these sources determines the necessary force structure.

The analysis begins with a breakdown of the United States' governing documents in order to determine the planned forces for the Pacific AOR in coming years. The main governing documents analyzed are the United States' *National Security Strategy*[60], the *National Military Strategy*[61] and the Chairman of the Joint Chiefs of Staff's (CJCS) Joint data used to determine unclassified force structures in the region. The next step in the analysis is a comparison of the types of forces available to the four strategic goals.

The forces in the USPACOM AOR available to align against the four strategic goals fall under the prevue of MARFORPAC, USARPAC, PACAF, PACFLT, and SOCPAC. These functional components are responsible for providing forces to meeting the Commander of USPACOM's intent in the region and the Philippines. Overall, the two main categories of forces for comparison are conventional versus special operations forces. Using the missions of USPACOM's functional component commands addresses the capabilities of the conventional and special operations forces in the Pacific. As an example, SOCPAC currently states the following on their website.

---

[60]White House, *National Security Strategy*.

[61]Department of Defense, *National Military Strategy*.

As a subordinate unified command of USPACOM, SOCPAC and its component units deploy throughout the Pacific, supporting USPACOM's Theater Security Cooperation Program, deliberate plans, and real world contingencies. SOCPAC elements annually conduct small unit exchanges, joint and combined training events, and operational deployments throughout the Pacific, fostering interoperability with host nation partners and facilitating strategic and operational objectives. Subordinate elements play a major role in ongoing counterdrug and humanitarian demining operations, training host nation forces in Thailand, Laos, Cambodia, Vietnam, the Philippines, and other Theater countries.[62]

Taking the force application from all of USPACOM's functional component commands into account, a comparison criteria rubric is necessary to use against the United States' strategic goals in the Philippines. Adding additional factors that enhance each functional component's ability to support the goals further separates each component's ability. The comparison rubric on a one to four scale shows the ability for each functional component. Table 1 shows how the final comparisons are determined and table 4 explained the comparison rubric. A comparison table provides ease of reading.

The first strategic goal is accelerating growth through improved competitiveness. According to the United States' Department of State, the areas of focus in this goal are investment and economic governance. These include the use of power, water, and wastewater services and contract enforcement and the rule of law.[63] These areas of focus, with their subcategories allow, for a method of determining conventional and special operations forces comparison on their ability to support this strategic goal.

The next strategic goal that the United States has in the Philippines is strengthening governance, rule of law, and the fight against corruption. This goal has two

---

[62]Special Operations Command, Pacific, "SOCPAC," http://www.socpac.socom. mil/default.aspx (accessed 1 July 2012).

[63]U.S. Mission to the Philippines, Appendix B.

areas of focus: judiciary and public finance. Under these focus areas, investigation and prosecution of human rights abuse cases and strengthening anti-corruption institutions are subcategories of concern.[64] This second strategic goal affords a stable Philippines and furthers the national objectives. On the outset, this goal and the previous goal do not align with United States military missions. However, in the "pivot to the Pacific,"[65] military activities might not be the best way to achieve United States' goals for the Philippines. Other national instruments of power such as diplomatic and economic might support these two goals in the Philippines.

The third strategic goal of the United States in the Philippines listed by the Department of State is investing in people to reduce poverty. This goal has some clear avenues where the United States military can be of assistance. The three focus areas of this goal are education, health, environment and disaster.[66] The ability of the United States to support disaster preparedness and facilitate engineering projects that provides water and sanitation is a key asset in this strategic goal. Moving forward in the analysis, finding the right combination of force necessary to support this goal leads to long- term progress and success for the Filipino people.

Promoting a peaceful and secure Philippines is the fourth goal that the United States has for its relationship with the Philippines. Currently, the United States supports this goal by conventional forces through the annual Balikatan[67] exercise and with special

---

[64]Ibid.

[65]Congressional Research Service.

[66]U.S. Mission to the Philippines, Appendix B.

[67]Pike.

operations forces within Joint Special Operations Task Force–Philippines.[68] The United States' Department of State lists the goal's focus areas as military forces and law enforcement.[69] Targeting insurgent organizations in the Philippine islands is paramount to the success of this goal for both the United States and the Philippines.

The following comparison chart aids in the analysis of the information in the United States' governing sources and the four strategic goals in the Philippines. This chart's purpose is to ascertain the best aligned force to support the four goals. This chart will be the basis of the conclusions found in chapter five of this paper. The final chart will look like the following, except computed scores.

Table 1.   Notional Conclusion Table

Functional Component Command	Department of State Goals (1=Fails, 2=Marginal, 3=Satisfactory, 4=Exceptional)					Additional Factors (0=no ability, 1=minimal, 2=substantial)				
	Accelerating Growth Through Increased Competitive-ness	Strengthening Governance, Rule of Law, & the Fight Against Corruption	Investing in People to Reduce Poverty	Promoting a Peaceful and Secure Philippines	Goals Total	Small Ground Unit Capability	Self-deploying Ability	Access to Culturally Trained Personnel	Factors Total	Overall Total
MARFOR PAC	A	B	C	D	W	Y	Y	Y	X	Z
PACFLT	E	F	G	H	W	Y	Y	Y	X	Z
PACAF	I	J	K	L	W	Y	Y	Y	X	Z
SOCPAC	M	N	O	P	W	Y	Y	Y	X	Z
USARPAC	Q	R	S	T	W	Y	Y	Y	X	Z

Source: Created by author.

---

[68]Joint Special Operations Task Force–Philippines, "JSOTF-P," http://www.jsotf-p.blogspot.com/ (accessed 2 July 2012).

[69]U.S. Mission to the Philippines, Appendix B.

This notional template is a way to determine the best-suited force to support the United States' strategic goals in the Philippines. This information leads to a solution as how to be support the Filipino people while achieving United States' strategy with American forces in the Pacific.

The next chapter of this paper analyzes the source documents in order to capture the information required to culminate the thesis. This analysis will focus on determining which is the best force, special operations forces or a conventional force.

CHAPTER 4

ANALYSIS

The last chapter focused on the methodology used to analyze the right type of United States' armed forces required to support the United States' strategic goals in the Philippines. What follows in this chapter is the analysis of the source documents described in chapter two in order to link a type of force, conventional or special operations force, to the four United States' strategic goals in the Philippines. Members of the United States' military serve abroad in support of United States' strategic goals across the globe. The American relationship with the Philippines has had difficult times and fruitful times for over a century.

Relationships between the two countries at this time are focusing on the future, not past problems, the goal being that the two nations can work together to further their own goals for Pacific region. In the Manila Declaration, signed in November 2011, the concluding paragraph speaks to the future.

> Sixty years on, the Philippines-United States alliance has never been stronger and will continue to expand in the 21st century as our two countries chart a new direction for our critical partnership, in the defense realm and beyond. Our common values, commitment to democracy and the rule of law, robust economic relationship, and strong people-to-people ties will continue to ensure that our partnership remains strong and vibrant well into the future. With an enduring history of shared sacrifice and common purpose, the people and governments of our two countries will act together to build a better and more prosperous world for future generations.[70]

---

[70]United States of America, Government of Republic of the Philippines, *Manila Declaration*.

Why United States Armed Forces are in the Philippines

Three main documents determine the relationship between the United States and the Philippines in terms of armed forces cooperation. Those documents are the Mutual Defense Treaty, signed in 1951, the visiting forces agreement, signed in 1998, and Manila Declaration, signed in 2011. These documents are the centerpiece in a relationship built on cooperation for common goals with respect to the Philippines.

The Mutual Defense Treaty was in response to Japanese aggression in World War II; however, some of the articles are applicable in today's environment. Article II states that the two countries "separately and jointly by self-help and mutual aid will maintain and develop their individual and collective capacity to resist armed attack."[71] The treaty defines armed attack as to "include an armed attack on the metropolitan territory of either of the parties, or on the island territories under its jurisdiction in the Pacific Ocean, its armed forces, public vessels or aircraft in the future."[72] The United States has been supporting the Armed Forces of the Philippines (AFP) in this manner as the AFP deals with internal threats and armed attacks from multiple terrorist organizations for over ten years. This current support links to the third United States' strategic goal in the Philippines, which deals with promoting a peaceful and secure Philippines.[73]

In order to provide any military support to the Filipino people the members of the United States military must abide by the policies of the visiting forces agreement with the

---

[71]United States of America, Republic of the Philippines, *Mutual Defense Treaty* (Washington, DC, 1951).

[72]Ibid.

[73]U.S. Mission to the Philippines, Appendix B.

Philippines. The visiting force agreement between the United States and the Philippines exists because "cooperation between the United States and the Republic of the Philippines promotes their common security interests."[74] The document outlines how American armed forces will gain entry into the Philippines, American treatment under Filipino law, how American equipment enters the country, and other aspects associated with American military support in the Philippines.[75] This information is imperative as American armed forces support the four United States' strategic goals in the Philippines.

The Manila Declaration is the most applicable to the four United States' strategic goals in the Philippines. The purpose of this newest document in a series of agreements on security is to "maintain a robust, balanced, and responsive security partnership including cooperating to enhance the defense, interdiction, and apprehension capabilities of the Armed Forces of the Philippines."[76] This purpose requires interaction between the United States armed forces and AFP in order to succeed. The document links the two nations in efforts to thwart not only armed attacks but other threats as well. The document states that the two countries are "determined to continue our bilateral cooperation in addressing broader regional and global challenges, including maritime security and threats to security such as climate change, nuclear proliferation, terrorism, and

---

[74]Government of the United States of America, Government of the Republic of the Philippines, *Regarding the Treatment of United States Armed Forces Visiting the Philippines* (Manila, Philippines, 1998).

[75]Ibid.

[76]United States of America, Government of Republic of the Philippines, *Manila Declaration.*

transnational crime. We are committed to continuing our close and effective cooperation to counter al-Qaida-linked terrorist groups in the southern Philippines."[77]

These statements not only speak to the United States' goal of promoting a peaceful and secure Philippines, but they also address the goal of accelerating growth through improved competitiveness.[78] Working with the Filipinos on agricultural projects and advances are activities that the United States armed forces can support in an effort to achieve the first United States' states strategic goal in the Philippines.

The Manila Declaration addresses the second United States goal of strengthening governance, rule of law, and the fight against corruption, as well as the third goal of investing in people to reduce poverty.[79] Both governments see these arenas as important focus areas in the coming years. The declaration contends the need to promote "great government transparency and the rule of law."[80] Members of the United States military can coordinate with local governmental officials in regards to transparency and with the Philippine National Police on effective ways to assure rule of law. These efforts directly support the United States' strategic goals in the Philippines. Furthermore, these efforts endeavor to give the Filipino people the ability to function in a safe and secure environment.

---

[77]Ibid.

[78]U.S. Mission to the Philippines, Appendix B.

[79]Ibid.

[80]United States of America, Government of Republic of the Philippines, *Manila Declaration.*

The document recognizes a pressing requirement to "reduce poverty by creating inclusive, sustainable economic growth in the Philippines."[81] Using United States' armed forces in poor areas in order to support civic action programs is necessary to accomplishing this goal. Working with local businesses to support local barangay (village) areas to support Filipinos employing Filipinos to build needed infrastructure aids in accomplishing this goal.

The United States and the Philippines signed a Mutual Logistics Support Agreement in November 2007. This document assures "further the interoperability, readiness, and effectiveness" of American and Filipino military forces "through increased logistic cooperation."[82] Colonel Romulo Supapo states that the real purpose of this agreement is to "lower the cost of security cooperation by minimizing administrative costs and waste."[83] The concept of a logistics linkage between the two nations is important. Allowing the United States a location further positioned across the Pacific enables the American military further flexibility of operations across the Pacific.

With these documents in place and addressing the military interaction between the United States and the Philippines, the question remains as to what is the right military force compliment to support the United States strategic goals in the Philippines. In order to determine the force needed, it is important to understand what forces are currently available in the Pacific.

---

[81]Ibid.

[82]Department of Defense of the United States of America and the Department of National Defense of the Republic of the Philippines, *Mutual Logistics Support Agreement* (Washington, DC, Manila, Philippines, 2007), 2.

[83]Supapo.

United States Armed Forces Currently in the Pacific

The forces in the Pacific are under the COCOM authority of USPACOM. These forces fall under the title of USPACOM's functional component commands. The functional components are USARPAC (United States Army), PACFLT (United States Navy), MARFORPAC (United States Marines), PACAF (United States Air Force), and SOCPAC (Special Operations Forces). Each functional component receives their forces from their corresponding service component with the exception being SOCPAC, whose receives forces from all four United States' service components. All of the forces assigned across the Pacific are located in places like Hawai'i, Alaska, Japan, Korea, and Guam.

USARPAC

"USARPAC conducts operations to assure, enhance, sustain, and influence military relationships that build partner defense capacity; prepare the force for unified land operations; respond to threats; sustain and protect the force; to shape and posture for a stable and secure U.S. Pacific Command area of responsibility."[84] USARPAC has thirteen active duty and major subordinate commands. Two of the subordinate commands, Eighth Army and U.S. Army Japan focus on enduring United States' relationships in the Pacific. Eighth Army resides on the Korean peninsula and supports the defense of the Republic of Korea, and U.S. Army Japan focuses on the United States' support to the people of Japan.[85]

---

[84]US Army Pacific, "Command Structure," http://www.army.mil/info/organization/unitsandcommands/commandstructure/usarpac/ (accessed 1 August 2012).

[85]Ibid.

Not only does USARPAC align its forces geographically, but they also align their forces functionally. This division of forces is necessary to accomplishing USARPAC's overall missions in the Pacific. Joint Task Force – Homeland Defense exists to "conduct Homeland Defense operations to deter threats to critical infrastructure and key resources and when requested/validated, conducts Civil Support operation in response to hazards to mitigate human suffering and reduce infrastructure damage."[86] The Fifth Battlefield Coordination Detachment "insures that the Joint Force Air Component Commander and Joint Air Operations Center are aware of the ARFOR [Army Force] Commander's intent, scheme of maneuver, and requirements for air support."[87] The soldiers of the Fifth Battlefield Coordination Detachment work on Hickam Air Force Base in the Thirteen Air Force air operations center. Additional units like the 8th Theater Sustainment Command, the 311th Theater Signal Command, the 18th Medical Command and the 500th Military Intelligence Brigade support Army operations with additional support assets across the Pacific. The 196th Infantry Brigade provides training and certification for Army components in the Pacific.[88]

The main maneuver elements for USARPAC, outside of Korea and Japan, are the 25th Infantry Division and U.S. Army Alaska. The 25th Infantry Division Commander's intent is that the 25th Infantry Division "will remain the Pacific Theater's decisive ground combat force from Platoon to Joint Task Force Headquarters." He continues to

---

[86]Joint Task Force–Homeland Defense, "Joint Task Force – Homeland Defense," http://www.usarpac.army.mil/docs/jtf-hd/ (accessed 1 August 2012).

[87]5th Battlefield Coordination Detachment, http://www.usarpac.army.mil/5thBCD/ (accessed 1 August 2012).

[88]US Army Pacific.

state that they are "prepared whether the situation requires lethal force, humanitarian assistance, building partner nation capacity or support to civil authorities."[89] According to their commander, "Tropic Lightning" Division is ready to support any operation in the Pacific.

The other large deployable force in the Pacific under USARPAC is in Alaska. These "Artic Warriors" state that they are USPACOM's "Strategic Response Force."[90] However, the strategic focus of the "Arctic Warriors" is the defense of Alaska. The mission of United States Army Alaska is that it "executes continuous training and readiness oversight responsibilities for ARFORGEN [Army Force Generation] in Alaska and supports U.S. Pacific Command's Theater Security Cooperation Program. On order, [United States Army Alaska] executes Joint Force Land Component Command functions in support of Homeland Defense and Security in Alaska."[91] Although these forces focus on Alaska, they can support USPACOM in the execution of its strategic plans in the Pacific.

The closest USARPAC force to support United States' strategic goals in the Philippines is the 25th Infantry Division. This force aligns to deploy to support USPACOM intent in the Philippines and does not have a dedicated mission for Homeland Defense, such as United States Army Alaska. USARPAC is not the only land component available for use by USPACOM.

---

[89]25 ID, 25th Infantry Division, "The Mission of the 25th Infantry Division," http://www.25idl.army.mil/mission.html (accessed 6 August 2012.)

[90]USARAK, *United States Army Alaska Pamphlet 600-2* (Joint Base Elmendorf-Richardson, AK, 2010), 3.

[91]Ibid., 11.

MARFORPAC

The other ground component in the Pacific AOR is MARFORPAC. According to the MARFORPAC structure, "MARFORPAC is the largest field command in the U.S. Marine Corps" and it has over 74,000 Marines and Sailors in its "peacetime combat force."[92] MARFORPAC is composed of two major force structures, called Marine Expeditionary Forces (MEF). Based in Hawai'i, I MEF "deploys and is employed as Marine Air Ground Task Force (MAGTF) in support of Combatant Command (COCOM) requirements for contingency response or Major Theater War."[93] The other MEF, III MEF, resides in Okinawa, Japan. The reason for this force is to support the security treaty between the United States and Japan. III MEF states that, "although home based on Okinawa, units and personnel here may often spend much of their time training in other countries, taking part in numerous exercises throughout the Pacific."[94]

Based on this information, I MEF seems to be the best force suited to support United States' strategic goals in the Philippines. III MEF's purpose is to support the security treaty between the United States and Japan. However, as shown above, III MEF does deploy its Sailors and Marines throughout the Pacific for training. In other words, III MEF personnel could deploy to the Philippines in support of Unites States' strategic interests. In order to move around the Pacific in significant numbers, MARFORPAC requires a fleet of ships to support deployment.

---

[92]United States Marine Corps, "United States Marine Forces, Pacific," http://www.marforpac.marines.mil/ (accessed 6 August 2012).

[93]Ibid.

[94]Ibid.

PACFLT

The ability to move across the Pacific comes from PACFLT. PACFLT's mission is to "protect[s] and defend[s] the collective maritime interests of the United States and its allies and partners in the Asia-Pacific region. In support of U.S. Pacific Command and with allies and partners, U.S. Pacific Fleet enhances stability, promotes maritime security and freedom of the seas, deters aggression and when necessary, fights to win."[95] In order to accomplish this mission, PACFLT has fourteen subordinate commands. MARFORPAC is a subordinate command under PACFLT because Marines fall under the Department of the Navy. The remaining thirteen subordinate organizations are numbered fleets, regional commands or based on a specific task.

The two numbered fleets in PACFLT are Seventh Fleet, stationed in Japan or Third Fleet, stationed in San Diego, California. The Philippines falls under Seventh Fleet's AOR. Seventh Fleet states "U.S. naval forces help encourage dialogue, promote growth and ensure free flow of trade."[96] This concept aligns to the United States' strategic goal of "accelerating growth through increase competitiveness."[97] Seventh Fleet has between 60-70 ships assigned at any given time and conducts up to 100 partner nation exercises and 250 port visits annually.[98] Seventh Fleet currently supports exercises and conduct port visits in the Philippines. Out of the two numbered fleets for PACFLT,

---

[95]PACFLT, "Commander, U.S. Pacific Fleet," http://www.cpf.navy.mil/ (accessed 6 August 2012).

[96]7th Fleet, "Commander, U.S. 7th Fleet," http://www.c7f.navy.mil/ (accessed 6 August 2012).

[97]U.S. Mission to the Philippines, Appendix B.

[98]7th Fleet.

Seventh Fleet would be the fleet of choice to support United States' strategic goals in the Philippines.

PACFLT has five subordinate commands focused on specific tasks. These tasks are naval air, naval surface, submarine, naval construction, and maritime defense. The purpose of the PACFLT Naval Air Force is to "man, train, equip and maintain a Naval Air Force that is immediately employable, forward deployed and engaged. We support the Fleet and Unified Commanders by delivering the right force with the right readiness at the right time with a reduced cost . . . today and in the future."[99] These forces can support United States' strategic goals in the Philippines if USPACOM required support such as intelligence, surveillance, and reconnaissance was part of its intent in the Philippines.

The Commander of Naval Surface Forces, PACFLT is "comprised of surface ships, and support and maintenance commands, provides operational commanders with well-trained, highly effective, and technologically superior surface ships and Sailors."[100] This command is responsible for all of the naval surface ships across the entire Pacific to include the two numbered fleets, the regional commands and the specific task surface ships. When USPACOM requires PACFLT to support its intent and the United States' strategic goals in the Philippines, PACFLT Naval Surface Forces supports those requirements.

---

[99]Naval Air Forces, "Commander, Naval Air Forces," http://www.cnaf.navy.mil/ (accessed 6 August 2012).

[100]Naval Surface Force, PACFT, "Commander, Naval Surface Force, U.S. Pacific Fleet," http://www.public.navy.mil/surfor/Pages/mission.aspx (accessed 6 August 2012).

If the United States has strategic interests that require subsurface support in the Pacific, Submarine Force U.S. Pacific Fleet supports the need. The Submarine "Force's mission is to provide the training, logistical plans, manpower and operational plans and support and tactical development necessary to maintain the ability of the Force to respond to both peacetime and wartime demands."[101] If there was a direct maritime threat to the Philippines, the forces from Submarine Force, PACFLT, could mitigate the threat to the Philippines.

The next specific task unit under PACFLT is the Maritime Defense Zone Pacific. These forces primarily belong to the United States Coast Guard and protect United States' entities and coastlines in the Pacific.[102] If required, they could support training of Filipino Coast Guard-like entities.

The final specific task subordinate command under PACFLT is the First Naval Construction Division. Their mission is to "provide public works support at Naval Support Activities, Forward Operating Bases and Fleet Hospital/Expeditionary Medical Facilities during wartime or contingency operations."[103] These "SEABEE" forces are perfect for supporting the United States' strategic goal of "investing in people to reduce

---

[101]Submarine Force, PACFLT, "Commander, Submarine Force U.S. Pacific Fleet," http://www.csp.navy.mil/about_us.shtml (accessed 6 August 2012).

[102]United States Coast Guard, "Pacific Area," http://www.uscg.mil/pacarea/ (accessed 6 August 2012).

[103]United States Navy Construction Force, "Welcome to the home of the SEABEES," http://www.seabee.navy.mil/ (accessed 6 August 2012).

poverty."[104] The SEABEEs can help build up local barangay and to develop Filipino military engineer capabilities.

On top of dividing their subordinate commands into numbered fleets and specific task organizations, PACFLT divided the Pacific into regions. Those regions are Japan, Korea, Marianas, Southwest, Northwest, and Hawai'i.[105] These regional commands are responsible for the support of any training in their region and ensuring compliance of all laws and regulations. The Philippines does not fall under a direct regional control of any regional commander and ships in the Philippines' national waters should rely on their home regional command for any support. An area for further research is the consideration of PACFLT creating a regional command for the Philippines.

PACFLT forces can have a major role in supporting any United States' activities in the Philippines. They can provide forces to support the Filipino people and ensure maritime protection of the Philippine islands. Furthermore, bilateral exercises between the United States Navy and the Filipino Navy assure advancement in the Filipino ability to protect their own shores. PACFLT can readily support three of the four United States' strategic goals in the Philippines. Those goals are "accelerating growth through improved competitiveness, investing in people to reduce poverty, and promoting a peaceful and secure Philippines."[106] PACFLT is not the only force capable of projecting United States' power across the Pacific. In the air domain, this projection falls under PACAF.

---

[104]U.S. Mission to the Philippines, Appendix B.

[105]PACFLT.

[106]U.S. Mission to the Philippines, Appendix B.

PACAF

PACAF's mission is "to provide ready air and space power to promote U.S interests in the Asia-Pacific region during peacetime, through crisis and in war." The PACAF AOR covers over 100 million square miles and include 44 countries.[107] PACAF divides its operational capabilities into numbered air forces. Those numbered air forces are the 5th, 7th, 11th and the 13th. Like USARPAC, MARFORPAC, and PACFLT, PACAF has forces aligned to specific countries or regions. Fifth Air Force supports treaties with Japan. Seventh Air Force supports treaties with Korea. Eleventh Air Force is in Alaska and supports defense of the United States' borders in Alaska.[108] Although these forces support specific locations, they can support United States' strategic goals in the Philippines.

If any air forces support United States' strategic goals in the Philippines, Thirteenth Air Force leverages them. The mission of Thirteenth Air Force is to "Plan, command, control, deliver, and assess air, space and information operations in the Asia-Pacific region. Conduct theater engagement to shape and enhance operational capability. Execute successful operations across the security spectrum from humanitarian assistance to major combat operations."[109] Thirteenth Air Force has forces located in Hawai'i and on rotation in Guam. Because the Thirteenth operates USPACOM's air operations center, they would be the designated unit to provide any airpower support to United States'

---

[107]PACAF, "Pacific Air Forces," http://www.pacaf.af.mil/ (accessed 6 August 2012).

[108]Ibid.

[109]13 AF, "13th Air Force," http://www.13af.pacaf.af.mil/units/index.asp (accessed 6 August 2012).

strategic goals in the Philippines. As such, PACAF forces are best suited to support the United States' strategic goal of "promoting a peaceful and secure Philippines."[110]

The conventional forces of USARPAC, MARFORPAC, PACFLT, and PACAF usually provide a large visual statement when they support United States' strategic objectives in the Pacific. When the United States wants to have a smaller visual signature, but still achieve a strategic effect, special operations forces are the preferred force.

SOCPAC

In the Pacific, special operations forces fall under the command of SOCPAC. As stated in Chapter 3, SOCPAC currently states the following on their website.

> As a subordinate unified command of USPACOM, SOCPAC and its component units deploy throughout the Pacific, supporting USPACOM's Theater Security Cooperation Program, deliberate plans, and real world contingencies. SOCPAC elements annually conduct small unit exchanges, joint and combined training events, and operational deployments throughout the Pacific, fostering interoperability with host nation partners and facilitating strategic and operational objectives. Subordinate elements play a major role in ongoing counterdrug and humanitarian demining operations, training host nation forces in Thailand, Laos, Cambodia, Vietnam, the Philippines, and other Theater countries.[111]

The forces assigned to SOCPAC come from three United States' service components. From the United States Army, SOCPAC has command over the 1-1st Special Forces Group in Okinawa, Japan. From the United States Navy, SOCPAC has command authority over Navy Special Warfare Unit One on the island of Guam. From the United States Air Force, SOCPAC has command authority over the 353rd Special Operations Group in Okinawa. SOCPAC also lists Joint Special Operations Task Force –

---

[110]U.S. Mission to the Philippines, Appendix B.

[111]Special Operations Command, Pacific.

Philippines (JSOTF-P) as a subordinate unit on their website.[112] As stated in Chapter 3, this unit is responsible for supporting Filipino forces in their efforts to combat insurgent terrorist organizations in the Southern Philippines.[113] These forces have the benefit of forward positioning across the Pacific in order to meet the requirements of USPACOM and USSOCOM.

SOCPAC states that its "forces are operating in multiple high-priority Pacific Theater countries, increasing partner nation capabilities to defeat international terrorism, improving cultural understanding, and fully prepared to meet emerging threats."[114] Based on these statements and the current JSOTF-P operations in the Philippines, SOCPAC is poised to support the United States' strategic goal of "promoting a peaceful and secure Philippines."[115]

The following table depicts the current United States' armed forces in the Pacific. Country/area listed below the unit's name depicts support to specific missions or treaties.

---

[112]Ibid.

[113]Joint Special Operations Task Force–Philippines.

[114]Special Operations Command, Pacific.

[115]U.S. Mission to the Philippines, Appendix B.

Table 2. Current United States' Armed Forces in the Pacific

USARPAC	MARFORPAC	PACFLT	PACAF	SOCPAC
Eighth Army (Korea)	I MEF	7th Fleet	5th Air Force (Japan)	1-1st Special Forces Group
25th Infantry Division	III MEF (Japan)	3rd Fleet	7th Air Force (Korea)	Navy Special Warfare Group 1
U.S. Army Alaska		Naval Air Force	11th Air Force (Alaska)	353 Special Operations Group
U.S. Army Japan		Naval Surface Force	13th Air Force	JSOTF-P (Philippines)
8th Theater Sustainment Command		Naval Submarine Force		
311th Theater Signal Command		Naval Construction Division Pacific		
94th Army Air Missile Defense Command		Maritime Defense Zone Pacific		
9th Mission Support Command		Naval Forces (Japan)		
196th Infantry Brigade		Naval Forces (Korea)		
500th Military Intelligence Brigade		Joint Region Marianas		
18th Medical Command		Navy Region Southwest		
Joint Task Force – Homeland Defense		Navy Region Northwest		
5th Battlefield Coordination Detachment		Navy Region Hawai'i		

Source: Created by author.

Each United States' armed service (Army, Navy, Marine Corps, Air Force) currently has forces assigned to support specific countries or areas. SOCPAC commands joint special operations task force established to support operations in the Philippines. The forces under the COCOM authority of USPACOM today exist to support the Commander of USPACOM's intent in the theater. Those forces are located and designed to support the *National Security Strategy* (NSS) and other past governing documents. The next section will look at the current governing documents and other sources to determine what the force structure of the Pacific in the near future.

Future United States Armed Forces in the Pacific

According to the USPACOM Strategic Guidance of 2011, "USPACOM will emphasize interagency alignment, especially within the Department of Defense and with the Department of State, and will support whole-of-government approaches to regional challenges and opportunities."[116] Admiral Willard, at that time Commander of USPACOM, wanted to achieve this through "continual forward presence enabled by an adaptive regional military posture."[117] In order to accomplish continual forward presence the United States' military needs to continue to have forces focused on the USPACOM mission. The United States' NSS helps determine the forces in the Pacific AOR.

The United States' NSS wants to "strengthen institutions and mechanisms for cooperation."[118] This goal is a guiding factor to determine the right military force structure across the globe. In order to provide "mechanisms for cooperation," the NSS wants to "invest in regional capabilities."[119] This investment affects the focus of all the COCOMs to include USPACOM. The focus is to develop military organizations with

---

[116]Willard, 3.

[117]Ibid., 1.

[118]White House, *National Security Strategy*.

[119]Ibid.

regional familiarity in order to ease cooperation between the United States and partner nation militaries.

The United States' Department of Defense analyzes its current force structure and issues a report about every four years called the *Quadrennial Defense Review* (QDR).[120] The most recent QDR from 2010, states that it "brings fresh focus to the importance of preventing and deterring conflict by working with and through allies and partners."[121] This focus aligns with the United States' efforts in the Philippines. In countries where the status of forces agreements does not allow large scale American forces, working with and through allies is paramount to success. The status of forces agreement between the United States and the Philippines does not state an exact number of American service members allowed on Filipino soil. In order to mitigate the possibility of conflict across the globe the QDR focuses on multiple efforts. The most applicable effort to current and future American forces in the Pacific is "enhancing U.S. capabilities to train, advise, and assist partner-nation security forces and contribute to coalition and peacekeeping operations."[122] Assisting partner-nation security forces is a way for the United States to further its counterterrorism and stability operations.

The QDR highlighted some areas where the United States needs to increase its capacity to conduct counterterrorism and stability operations. Two proposed increases can have an effect on the USPACOM forces support of the United States' strategic

---

[120]Department of Defense, *Quadrennial Defense Review* (Washington, DC: Department of Defense, 2010).

[121]Ibid., 1.

[122]Ibid., 13

49

objectives in the Philippines. The first increase is in "COIN [counter insurgency], stability operations, and CT [counterterrorism] competency and capacity in general purpose forces."[123] In the Pacific AOR, this means that forces outside of SOCPAC will get a boost in their ability to conduct these types of operations. That could mean MARFORPAC and USARPAC forces can get an unknown increase in capability.

The second proposed increase is to "expand the civil affairs capacity."[124] SOCPAC has access to civil affairs forces that are worldwide deployable under USSOCOM. Recently, the United States' Army increased its civil affairs capacity by adding a conventional force unit. According to the QDR, civil affairs units are important because they "assist partner governments in the rule of law, economic stability, governance, public health and welfare, infrastructure, and public education and information."[125] This capability supports all four of the United States' strategic goals in the Philippines. Therefore an increase in the American military's ability to conduct civil affairs will support USPACOM's efforts in accomplishing its goals for the Philippines.

The QDR asserts that increasing partner nation securities capabilities in important to assuring global progress. The 6th Special Operations Squadron, which falls under USSOCOM, is specifically addressed in the QDR as an area of increase. The QDR plans the "purchase of light, fixed wing aircraft"[126] to assure that the 6th Special Operations Squadron can meet the growing demands of partner nation requirements for fixed-wing

---

[123]Ibid., 24.

[124]Ibid.

[125]Ibid.

[126]Ibid., 30.

capability training. Although this squadron does not report directly to SOCPAC, members of the 6th Special Operations Squadron deploy to JSOTF-P to train AFP pilots.

Any increase in capability of the American military strives to meet COCOM initiatives and plans across the globe. The QDR addresses the importance of the regions of the globe and each region's focus. The QDR states that, "in Southeast Asia, we are working to enhance our long-standing alliances with Thailand and the Philippines."[127] In order to enhance current relationships, America finds it important to address its stance across the globe. The QDR states that in the next five years (i.e. 2010-2015), the United States will "work with allies and key partner to ensure a peaceful and secure Asia-Pacific region."[128] Obviously, American interests and goals need to align with their partner nations across the globe to be successful.

The Pacific region is no different from any other region in regards to goal alignment. Most countries prefer a stable and security regional environment in order for their citizens to flourish. In the Pacific, the United States plans to "augment and adapt our forward presence, which reassures allies of the U.S. commitment to their security."[129] As stated earlier in this chapter, American and Filipino agreements tie the security of both nations together. This augmentation can bring additional forces into the USPACOM AOR, which could be able to support the United States' strategic goals in the Philippines.

The overarching defense strategy of the United States is to "prevent and deter conflict." The QDR states that, "preventing the rise of threats to U.S. interests requires

---

[127]Ibid., 59.

[128]Ibid., 64.

[129]Ibid., 65.

the integrated use of diplomacy, development, and defense, along with intelligence, law enforcement, and economic tools of statecraft, to help build the capacity of partners to maintain and promote stability." [130] This statement aligns with the how the United States' armed forces will be able to support the four United States' strategic goals in the Philippines. According to American military leaders, merging all of the United States' capabilities across its national instruments of power is the best process to prevent and deter conflict.

The United States' military takes the strategic guidance from the NSS and QDR, and uses it as one of the sources to develop its *National Military Strategy* (NMS). The NMS states that one of the United States' "enduring national interests" is "an international order advanced by U.S. leadership that promotes peace, security, and opportunity through stronger cooperation to meet global challenges."[131] USPACOM conducts this strategy through its efforts across the Pacific and in the Philippines. The cooperation can be through cultural exchanges, exercises, partnered operations, humanitarian assistance and countless other mechanisms. USPACOM's efforts must also meet American military objectives.

United States' military leadership develops these national American objectives by using the NSS and QDR as a guide. According to the NMS, the current American "national military objectives" are to counter violent extremism; deter and defeat aggression; strengthen international and regional security; [and] shape the future

---

[130]Ibid., v.

[131]Department of Defense, *National Military Strategy*, 4.

force."[132] USPACOM follows the first three objects with its support of the four United States' strategic goals in the Philippines. The fourth objective requires USPACOM to coordinate with the military leaders of each armed service to garner the forces necessary to meet the objectives. The QDR and NMS lead to increases in some capabilities and decreases in some capabilities across the American military in order to accomplish national and military objectives.

Like the NSS and the QDR, the NMS focuses on certain global regions. The NMS stresses the importance of the Pacific region to United States' national interests. Furthermore, like the NSS and QDR, the NMS addresses an increase in focus in the USPACOM AOR.

> We will expand our military security cooperation, exchanges, and exercises with the Philippines, Thailand, Vietnam, Malaysia, Pakistan, Indonesia, Singapore, and other states in Oceania – working with them to address domestic and common foreign threats to their nation's integrity and security. This will also help ensure we maintain a sustainable and diversified presence and operational access in the region. Lastly, we strongly encourage the development of security ties and commitments that are emerging among our allies and partners in the region. This helps strengthen regional norms and demonstrates increase responsibility and cooperation in addressing regional security challenges.[133]

Any expansion of cooperation with the Philippines could require an increase in forces available to USPACOM. These forces would then align to the United State' objectives in the region and could support the four United States' strategic goals in the Philippines. If there is an expansion of forces in the Pacific, finding the right location to house the new personnel is important and an area for further research.

---

[132]Ibid.

[133]Ibid., 14.

One of the best assets to support partner nations is having a cultural understanding of nation that a force is supporting. This has proven true in many American activities across the globe. Because of this experience, American military leaders addressed this cultural understanding in *Joint Vision 2020*. They stated, "A deep understanding of the cultural, political, military, and economic characteristics of a region must be established and maintained. Developing this understanding is dependent upon shared training and education, especially with key partners, and may require organizational change as well."[134] The United States' military has been stressing language training across each service. This has been a constant in American SOF, but language training has not been a constant in American conventional forces.

One service, the United States' Army, is not only stressing language training, but also are conducting "organizational change." On 16 May 2012, Army Chief of Staff General Ray Odierno stated, "The Army will begin implementing a regionally-aligned force concept next year [2013] to better support combatant commanders."[135] The goal is to provide COCOM commanders a regionally trained capability to meet their strategic intent. Speculation is that could be as many as six regionally aligned units assigned to USPACOM.[136] These proposed USPACOM aligned forces may not reside in the USPACOM AOR. They might reside in the continental United States and be deployed to

---

[134]Joint Chiefs of Staff, *Joint Vision 2020*, 17.

[135]Rob McIlvaine, "Odierno: Regional alignments to begin next year," *U.S. Army*, http://www.army.mil/article/79919 (accessed 8 August 2012).

[136]Michelle Tan, "Army now reorganizing geographically," *Army Times*, http://www.armytimes.com/news/2012/06/army-transitions-war-reorganizing-geographically-063012w/ (accessed 8 August 2012).

the USPACOM AOR when needed to support the USPACOM commander's intent in the Pacific AOR. These new units could bolster USPACOM's capability to support the following United States' strategic goals in the Philippines.

United States' Strategic Goals in the Philippines

In order to understand the United States' armed force that is best suited to support the United States' strategic goals in the Philippines, explanation of the goals is important. The United States' Department of State is responsible for furthering its global goals. The Department of State mission statement is to "shape and sustain a peaceful, prosperous, just, and democratic world and foster conditions for stability and progress for the benefit of the American people and people everywhere."[137]

The United States of America provided an estimated $142,435,000 in 2012 and requested $144,432,000 in aid for 2013. This money executes through programs like the foreign aid account and foreign military financing. This does not include the $434,000,000 Millennium Challenge contract the United States signed with the GRP in 2010. [138] The United States' Department of State must assure that the execution of these funds occur properly as they are a method of United States policy in the Philippines.

The United States' Department of State also develops a strategy with each country that it exchanges relationships. The Philippines is not different in this regard. Each Chief of Mission assigned to a country under the United States' State Department must accomplish the United States' strategy about their country of assignment. The "Country

---

[137]United States Department of State, "United States Department of State," http://www.state.gov/s/d/rm/index.htm#mission (accessed 7 August 2012).

[138]Lum, 12.

Assistance Strategy: Philippines"[139] is the name of the United States' Department of State strategy for the Philippines.

The current strategy looks at a period from 2009 until 2013. The twenty-five document outlines the United States' strategic interests in the Philippines. This strategy states that the "central U.S. foreign policy goal is that the Philippines becomes a more stable, prosperous and well-governed nation that is no longer a haven for terrorists."[140] Of course, many people and organizations have different definitions of the word terrorists and therefore terrorism. For the purpose of this paper, terrorists are individuals that conduct terrorism. Terrorism is "premeditated, politically motivated violence perpetrated against noncombatant targets by subnational groups or clandestine agents, usually intended to influence an audience."[141] The Department of State strategy further states "strategic vision of the U.S. foreign assistance in the Philippines is a more prosperous, well-governed and stable democracy that is able to meet the needs of its people, especially the poor."[142] These two statements nest with the United States National Security interest of "disrupt[ing], dismantle[ing], and defeat[ing] Al-Qa'ida and its violent extremist affiliates in the Afghanistan, Pakistan, and around the world."[143]

---

[139]U.S. Mission to the Philippines.

[140]Ibid., 2.

[141]U.S. Department of State, Office of the Coordinator for Counterterrorism, "Chapter 7–Legislative Requirements and Key Terms," http://www.state.gov/j/ct/rls/crt/2007/103715.htm (accessed 21 September 2012).

[142]Ibid., 3.

[143]White House, *National Security Strategy*, 19.

Dealing with terrorists falls under one of the strategic goals that the United States has for the Philippines. According to the United States' Department of State "Country Assistance Strategy" for the Philippines, the United States has four goals in the Philippines. Those goals are accelerating growth through improved competitiveness; strengthening governance, rule of law, and the fight against corruption; investing in people to reduce poverty; and promoting a peaceful and secure Philippines.[144] These goals are further broken down by assistance approaches, areas of focus and cross-cutting themes. The table below is Appendix B of the United States' Department of State Country Assistance Strategy for the Philippines.

Table 3.   United States' Strategic Goals in the Philippines

Vision. A more prosperous, well-governed and stable democracy that is able to meet the needs of its people, especially the poor

Priority Goals			
Accelerating Growth through Improved Competitiveness	Strengthening Governance, Rule of Law, and the Fight against Corruption	Investing in People to Reduce Poverty	Promoting a Peaceful and Secure Philippines
Assistance Approaches			
➤ Improve infrastructure provision ➤ Streamline business procedures ➤ Increase efficiency of tax and customs administration ➤ Reduce barriers to market entry ➤ Enhance effectiveness of regulation and enforcement ➤ Strengthen property rights ➤ Reduce energy costs ➤ Expand workforce development for youth and adults	➤ Improve fiscal management and revenue generation ➤ Increase judicial efficiency, competence, and integrity ➤ Reduce corruption ➤ Improve human rights protection and trafficking systems ➤ Strengthen electoral institutions and systems	➤ Increase access for children and youth to quality education ➤ Reduce geographic disparities in health conditions ➤ Increase household access to water and sanitation services ➤ Reduce threats to biodiversity resources ➤ Increase effectiveness of disaster preparedness and relief programs	➤ Mitigate criminal and terrorist activities, especially in Mindanao ➤ Strengthen Philippine military systems and personnel resources ➤ Improve Philippine law enforcement institutions
Areas of Focus			
Investment ➤ Improved transportation and logistics ➤ Microenterprise growth ➤ Agricultural productivity ➤ Youth employability ➤ Provision of power, water, and wastewater services Economic governance ➤ Tax & customs administration reform ➤ Contract enforcement and the rule of law ➤ Local implementation of reform programs	Judiciary ➤ Alternative dispute resolution, improved court procedures, legal education reform ➤ Philippine Judicial Academy strengthening ➤ Investigation and prosecution of human rights abuse cases Public finance ➤ Budget oversight improvement ➤ Revenue forecasting ➤ Institutional linkages between national and local governments ➤ Anti-corruption institutions strengthening	Education ➤ Access to quality of basic education for children Health ➤ Health sector governance ➤ Equitable access to services ➤ Private sector contribution to public health outcomes Environment and disaster ➤ National and local natural resource management capacities ➤ Water and sanitation systems and approaches ➤ Disaster preparedness	Military ➤ Philippine Defense Reform ➤ Counterterrorism efforts through training and equipping Philippine forces ➤ Modernization of the Armed Forces of the Philippines based on U.S. systems ➤ Respect for human rights and the rule of law Law enforcement ➤ Capacity to address terrorism and criminal activities.
Cross-Cutting Themes			
Governance and Rule of Law: Emphasis on human rights, anti-corruption, effective administration of justice, and provision of services by local governments. Conflict Reduction in Mindanao: Focus on conflict-affected areas in Mindanao, given poverty, major development and security challenges. Disadvantaged and Vulnerable Populations: Address concerns of the poor, women and children, victims of trafficking and human rights abuses at serious risk from economic events, food insecurity, violent conflict, natural disasters, environmental degradation and climate change. Disaster Preparedness and Mitigation: Improve capabilities to mitigate and respond to natural disasters. Public-Private Partnerships: Leverage assistance investments with other government and non-government partners as a fundamental business practice.			

Source: U.S. Mission to the Philippines, *Country Assistance Strategy Philippines: 2009-2013* (Washington, DC: Department of State, 2009), Appendix B

---

[144]U.S. Mission to the Philippines, Appendix B.

These goals are the baseline to compare the types of United States' armed forces required to support United States' strategic goals in the Philippines. Understanding the available capabilities of the United States' armed forces and the proposed Pacific forces in the near future, answers the question as to what is the right type of force to support these goals.

The first goal is accelerating growth through improved competitiveness. According to the Department of State, the American program areas for this goal are "macroeconomic foundation for growth, trade and investment, financial sector, infrastructure, agriculture, private sector competitiveness, economic opportunity, and energy."[145] Although this goal is not inherently military, the United States' armed forces can help the Filipinos build and plan infrastructure and teach agriculture techniques to the Filipinos. Using PACFLT's naval construction teams and SOCPAC's civil affairs personnel furthers this United States' strategic goal. In order to have accelerated growth in the Philippines, the GRP must mitigate corruption and maintain rule of law.

The second goal is strengthening governance, rule of law, and the fight against corruption. According to the Department of State, the American program areas for this goal are "transnational crime, conflict mitigation and reconciliation, rule of law and human rights, and good governance."[146] According to an independent study, during the last Filipino presidency, "human rights groups accused Philippine security forces – the AFP and Philippine National Police – and their proxies of carrying out extrajudicial

---

[145]U.S. Mission to the Philippines, 4.

[146]Ibid.

killings of civilians."[147] These activities were seen as politically motivated activities at the local and national level. The United States' Navy can mitigate transnational crime. Forces from USARPAC and MARFORPAC can deploy to train AFP personnel on human rights. SOCPAC personnel can support good governance practices and conflict resolution in JSOTF-P AOR.

The third United States' strategic goal is investing in people to reduce poverty. The United States' focus areas for accomplishing this goal are "education, health, environment, water and sanitation, disaster assistance and readiness."[148] All of USPACOM's functional components can support this strategic goal. PACFLT and MARFORPAC can be on the ground following a natural disaster when the GRP requests American support. USARPAC forces will require PACFLT or PACAF support to gain access to the Philippines in order to support a natural disaster. PACAF can fly aircraft to the Philippines loaded with needed supplies following a natural disaster. SOCPAC forces can and have supported disasters in the Philippines. All USPACOM forces can support disaster response readiness training at the request of the GRP.

The final United States' strategic goal in the Philippines is promoting a peaceful and secure Philippines. The Department of State focus areas are "counter-terrorism, stabilization operations, and security sector reform."[149] Although all of USPACOM's functional components can support this goal, currently SOCPAC has the priority of focus on the goal. Although SOF should not have an enduring presence, SOCPAC forces have

---

[147]Lum, 6-7.

[148]Ibid., 5.

[149]Ibid.

conducted counter terrorism operations in the southern Philippines since January 2002.[150]

However, SOCPAC can leverage the capabilities of USARPAC, MARFORPAC,

PACFLT, and PACAF in order to accomplish its mission in the Philippines.

Filipino National Security Policy

When discussing American strategic goals concerning the Philippines, it is

important to consider the GRP's goals with respect to its nation. The GRP uses seven

elements of national security. These elements are socio-political stability, territorial

integrity, economic solidarity, ecological balance, cultural cohesiveness, moral-spiritual

consensus, peace, and harmony.[151] When referring to the United States in the GRP's

2011-2016 National Security Policy, they state, "a continuing US security presence in the

Asia Pacific is considered as a positive stabilizing force. Consequently, the 1951 RP-US

Mutual Defense Treaty (MDT) continues to remain relevant to this day." The GRP sees

the "United States' strategic interests in the West Philippine Sea [to] include freedom of

navigation and peaceful resolution of conflict."[152]

The GRP states that as a "matter of policy, the State shall undertake the necessary

steps to ensure that the Filipino National Community's welfare, well-being, ways of life,

institutions, territorial integrity and sovereignty are enhanced and protected."[153] In order

to achieve this policy, the GRP has two national security goals. Those two goals are to

---

[150]Special Operations Command, Pacific.

[151]Government of the Republic of the Philippines, *National Security Policy: 2011-2016 –Securing the Gains of Democracy* (Manila, Philippines: GRP, 2011), 4-6.

[152]Ibid., 12.

[153]Ibid., 24.

"promote internal socio-political stability" and to "capacitate the Philippines to exercise full sovereignty over its territory and to provide protection to its maritime and other strategic interests."[154]

Both of the GRP's national security goals align with the four United States' strategic goals in the Philippines. For example, under the GRP's goal of "promote internal socio-political stability," a focus area is to "strengthen the integrity of national institutions and promote good governance."[155] This subcategory aligns with the second United States' strategic goal in the Philippines of "strengthening governance, rule of law, and fight against corruption."[156] Under the second GRP strategic goal, there is a subcategory goal to "enhance our cooperative security arrangements with allies and neighbors." The GRP see "the continuation of its harmonious relationship with the United States as beneficial to its security and reaffirms this alliance with a view that US military presence is a major stabilizing factor in the region."[157] This second GRP strategic goal and statement align with the fourth United States goal of "promoting a peaceful and secure Philippines."[158]

The GRP's National Security Policy goes on to state that the "Philippines must enhance its cooperation arrangements with ASEAN [Association of Southeast Asian

---

[154]Ibid., 24-29.

[155]Ibid., 26.

[156]U.S. Mission to the Philippines, Appendix B.

[157]Government of the Republic of the Philippines, *National Security*, 30.

[158]U.S. Mission to the Philippines, Appendix B.

Nations] member countries, Japan, China, South Korea and Australia."[159] This is
important to understand as Americans because the GRP does not see the United States as
its only ally in the Pacific.

Other Countries' Interests

Based on the location in the Pacific, many countries have interests in the
Philippines. As stated in the second chapter, Australia "has developed bilateral security
dialogues" with the Philippines to include signing a counterterrorism memorandum
between the two nations in the past year.[160] Japan has even provided aid packages to the
Filipino people in Mindanao.[161] Additional American military presence in the Philippines
does not threaten some countries in the Pacific. The Indonesian government sees
American service members in the Philippines supporting counterterrorism operations as a
"domestic problem."[162]

Some scholars recommend revisiting the current treaties between Thailand the
Philippines because they are "out of date and exclusionary." Frank Miller proposes,
"Washington should seek stronger security relations with the region through the ASEAN
[Association of Southeast Asian Nations] Regional Forum." Mr. Miller's concept is that

---

[159]Government of the Republic of the Philippines, *National Security.*

[160]Simon.

[161]Ibid., 7.

[162]Anthony L. Smith, "Reluctant Partner: Indonesia's Response to U.S. Security
Policies," *Asia-Pacific Responses to U.S. Security Policies* (March 2003): 32.

other regional countries accept the expansion and that Australia should consider this approach as well.[163]

<u>Analyzing Current United States' Military Capabilities</u>
<u>Supporting Strategic Goals</u>

Overall, the United States' armed forces in the Pacific under the COCOM authorities of USPACOM have an important role in assuring the United States can accomplish its goals in the Philippines. Discerning which type of force is best suited to support these American goals is necessary to American strategic success.

The current forces assigned to USPACOM are able to support most American strategic goals across the Pacific. As shown, the American government positions its forces across the globe in order to implement global requirements for United States' citizens. USPACOM forces are no different and each functional service component provides varying levels of support to United States' strategic goals in the Philippines.

The analysis of each functional component's ability to support each goal comes from table 4. The comparison provides four levels of support that are fails to support, provides marginal support, provides satisfactory support, or provides exceptional support. The required support mechanisms come from table 3.

---

[163]Frank L. Miller, Jr., *Impact of Strategic Culture on U.S. Policies for East Asia* (Carlisle, PA: Strategic Studies Institute, 2003), 13.

Table 4.   Goal Support Comparison Criteria Rubric

Goal	Score Value			
	1	2	3	4
Accelerating Growth Through Increased Competitiveness	**Fails to support the goal** Very little ability to improve transportation and logistics infrastructure; support the provision of power, water and sanitation services; and contract support	**Marginal ability to support the goal** Some ability to improve transportation and logistics infrastructure; support the provision of power, water and sanitation services; and contract support	**Satisfactory ability to support the goal** Personnel with the ability to improve transportation and logistics infrastructure; support the provision of power, water and sanitation services; and contract support	**Exceptional ability to support the goal** Complete units with ability to improve transportation and logistics infrastructure; support the provision of power, water and sanitation services; and contract support
Strengthening Governance, Rule of Law, and the Fight Against Corruption	**Fails to support the goal** Very little ability to provide alternative dispute resolution, improved court proceedings, legal education reform; investigation into human rights abuses; budget oversight; anti-corruption support	**Marginal ability to support the goal** Some ability to provide alternative dispute resolution, improved court proceedings, legal education reform; investigation into human rights abuses; budget oversight; anti-corruption support	**Satisfactory ability to support the goal** Personnel with the ability to provide alternative dispute resolution, improved court proceedings, legal education reform; investigation into human rights abuses; budget oversight; anti-corruption support	**Exceptional ability to support the goal** Complete units with ability to provide alternative dispute resolution, improved court proceedings, legal education reform; investigation into human rights abuses; budget oversight; anti-corruption support
Investing in People to Reduce Poverty	**Fails to support the goal** Very little ability to improve health sector; water and sanitation provision; and disaster preparedness	**Marginal ability to support the goal** Some ability to improve health sector; water and sanitation provision; and disaster preparedness	**Satisfactory ability to support the goal** Personnel with the ability to improve health sector; water and sanitation provision; and disaster preparedness	**Exceptional ability to support the goal** Complete units with ability to improve health sector; water and sanitation provision; and disaster preparedness
Promoting a Peaceful and Secure Philippines	**Fails to support the goal** Very little ability to provide counterterrorism support; mitigate terrorism and criminal activity in Mindanao; and strengthen AFP systems and personnel	**Marginal ability to support the goal** Some ability to provide counterterrorism support; mitigate terrorism and criminal activity in Mindanao; and strengthen AFP systems and personnel	**Satisfactory ability to support the goal** Personnel with the ability to provide counterterrorism support; mitigate terrorism and criminal activity in Mindanao; and strengthen AFP systems and personnel	**Exceptional ability to support the goal** Complete units with ability to provide counterterrorism support; mitigate terrorism and criminal activity in Mindanao; and strengthen AFP systems and personnel

Source: Created by author.

Having additional identifiers adds value to each functional components score. In this analysis, values increase for small ground unit capability, self-deploying capability and the ability to access culturally trained personnel in support of operations in the Philippines. Each functional component receives a zero score if they have minimal ability in the additional identifier. If a functional component has a marginal capability in the additional identifier, they receive a score of one for that identifier. Finally, if a functional component has substantial ability in the identifier, they receive a score of two.

It is necessary to have a small ground unit capability because of existing force agreements and Filipino sensitivities to large forces on Filipino soil. The visiting force agreement outlines how American armed forces will gain entry into the Philippines, American treatment under Filipino law, how American equipment enters the country, and other aspects associated with American military support in the Philippines. It does not state the total number of American forces allowed in the Philippines.[164]

The reason why self-deploying capabilities are important relates to the location of the Philippines. As shown in figures one and two in chapter one, the Pacific is a large area and the Philippines as a nation composed for thousands of islands. In order to support the United States' strategic goals in the Philippines, American military forces have to be able to move a force to the Philippines. The forward projection capabilities category is second most important category in terms of the American military capability to support the United States' strategic goals in the Philippines.

---

[164]Government of the United States of America, Government of the Republic of the Philippines.

The final additional identifier is the ability to access culturally trained personnel. Every nation in the world has a unique culture. According to the Filipino Association of Stevens Tech, Filipinos have twenty typical habits. Some of the twenty are applicable to American military interaction in the Philippines. The first applicable Filipino trait is that "Filipinos are known to always run late." From an American military perspective, this is a very important point. Most Americans believe in punctuality and find tardiness to be offensive. Another Filipino trait important in this study is that "Filipinos are very family oriented"[165] Because Filipinos are family oriented, they tend to be open about their families and discuss everything with their extended families. This familiar interaction leads to operational security concerns from an American military perspective. Not every USPACOM functional component has ready access to personnel with Filipino cultural training.

The analysis of each functional component's additional factor abilities comes from table 5. The comparison provides three levels of capability that are no capability, minimal capability and substantial capability concerning the additional factor. The required support mechanisms come from table 3.

---

[165]Filipino Association of Stevens Tech, *About the Filipino Lifestyle*, Stevens Institute of Technology, http://www.stevens.edu/fast/culture.html (accessed 25 September 2012).

Table 5.   Additional Factors Rubric

Additional Factor	Score Value		
	0	1	2
Small Ground Unit Capability	**No capability with this additional factor** No small ground unit capability; requires existing ground unit support	**Minimal capability with this additional factor** Minimal ability to organize into small units; requires additional ground unit support	**Substantial capability with this additional factor** Substantial ability to organize into small ground units; ground units are self-sustaining for short durations
Self-deploying Ability	**No capability with this additional factor** No ability to deploy from unit home location to the Philippines without outside support	**Minimal capability with this additional factor** Minimal ability to deploy from unit home location to the Philippines; requires long haul logistics support for major unit movement	**Substantial capability with this additional factor** Substantial ability to deploy from unit home location to the Philippines without outside the organization assistance
Access to Culturally Trained Personnel	**No capability with this additional factor** No unit focused culture training	**Minimal capability with this additional factor** Minimal unit focused cultural training that prepares personnel for cultural immersion	**Substantial capability with this additional factor** Substantial unit focused cultural training that prepares personnel for cultural immersion

Source: Created by author.

This analysis focused on American interests in the Philippines, the American military forces under USPACOM, current United States' strategic documents and future USPACOM force availability. This information provides a basis to determine the right type of American forces needed in the Philippines. The conclusions analyze the forces available to USPACOM to support the United States' strategic goals and determine the best force to support those goals.

CHAPTER 5

CONCLUSIONS AND RECOMMENDATIONS

Conclusions

It is important to understand that the United States of America uses its military forces to further its strategic goals across the globe. As such, each COCOM is the focus of effort for its own AOR. In the Pacific, the United States COCOM is USPACOM. The functional components of USPACOM: MARFORPAC, USARPAC, PACFLT, PACAF, and SOCPAC all serve vital roles in furthering, not only the USPACOM Commander's intent in the Pacific, but also the United States' strategic goals in the Pacific. The Philippines is no different in this regard. All five of USPACOM's functional component commands are necessary to meet American strategic goals in the Philippines. Each subordinate command has strengths and weaknesses in regards to their abilities to support the four United States' strategic goals in the Philippines.

Goal 1: Accelerating Growth Through Improved Competitiveness

This goal focuses on investment and economic governance. Under investment, the United States' Department of State sees "improved transportation and logistics" and "provision of power, water, and wastewater services" as important areas of attention. Under the focus area of "economic governance," the Department of State focuses its efforts on "contract enforcement and the rule of law."[166] Table 4 shows the rubric for a score of one to four for each functional component based on its ability to improve

---

[166]U.S. Mission to the Philippines, Appendix B.

transportation and logistics infrastructure; support the provision of power, water and sanitation services; and contract support.

MARFORPAC's ability to support this goal also receives a score of three. Because the Marines are a light force with few organic engineering assets, improving Filipino transportation, logistics, power, water, and wastewater services across large areas is difficult. However, MARFORPAC's ability to use Marines in small units enables them to support customs administration reform. MARFORPAC forces can support customs inspections at supply ports. These trained personnel provide satisfactory support to this goal.

PACFLT's ability to support goal 1 is exceptional and they receive a score of four for this goal. PACFLT SEABEEs are a excellent capability that can enable their ability to support this goal.[167] SEABEE sailors have the proper training and skill sets to rapidly deploy and support Filipino construction projects and infrastructure improvements. Furthermore, PACFLT lawyers, like their other functional component counterparts, can support reform of taxes and customs administration.[168]

PACAF Airmen can support improved logistics and customs operations at Filipino airfields. PACAF has subordinate engineering squadrons that can provide localized engineering support and specialized engineering units able to support larger projects like airfield development. PACAF's contracting squadrons can provide contract support expertise to the GRP. These personnel can provide satisfactory support to this

---

[167]United States Navy Construction Force.

[168]U.S. Mission to the Philippines, Appendix B.

goal and therefore PACAF receives a score of three for its ability to provide assistance to goal 1.

Because of the size of USARPAC forces and their ability to support engineering projects with existing unit engineering assets, their ability to support this goal is satisfactory and they receive a score of three. USARPAC soldiers can support customs reform at local levels with military police support.

SOCPAC's current ability to support this goal receives a score of three. SOCPAC forces typically support localized military concerns and train host nation military forces. However, SOCPAC civil affairs personnel can work with Filipino engineering companies to provide them training on improving methods in transportation and provision of essential services. Like the other functional components, SOCPAC's lawyers can provide contract support.

Overall, the USPACOM functional component command best suited to support the United States' strategic goal of "accelerating growth through improved competitiveness" is PACFLT. [169] PACFLT's SEABEEs gives them an edge over the other functional component commands for this strategic goal. A graphic depiction of the results of this strategic goal comparison is at table 5.

Goal 2: Strengthening Governance, Rule of Law, and the Fight Against Corruption

This goal focuses on "judiciary" and "public finance." The United States' Department of State sees "alternate dispute resolution, improved court procedure, legal education reform" and the need to "strengthen electoral institutions and systems" as some

---

[169]Ibid.

of the important areas of attention. Under the focus area of "economic governance," the Department of State focuses its efforts on "contract enforcement and the rule of law."[170] Table 4 shows the rubric for a score of one to four for each functional component based on its ability to provide alternative dispute resolution, improved court proceedings, legal education reform; investigation into human rights abuses; budget oversight; anti-corruption support.

MARFORPAC's ability to support goal 2 is marginal because they lack personnel in great numbers necessary to cause an impact with respect to this goal. The Marines in the Pacific have some personnel capable of providing support in the legal arena, but they exist across the command. This marginal support ability gives MARFORPAC a score of two from the rubric.

PACFLT receives a score of three because it has a satisfactory ability to support goal 2. Navy lawyers can come from across the command to facilitate legal improvements. Also, because the Philippines is a large nations with thousands miles of coastline and territorial waters, knowledge of maritime law plays an important role in the priorities of the GRP.

PACAF also has a satisfactory ability to support this goal and receives a score of three. PACAF lawyers and contracting officers can provide tremendous insight into contractual law, anti-corruption policies and legal education. Like the other functional components, PACAF personnel can support other American governmental organizations with this expertise.

---

[170]Ibid.

SOCPAC, like MARFORPAC, has a marginal ability to support this goal and receives a score of two. Like the first goal, SOCPAC's civil affairs forces provide the best capability to support this goal. However, these forces are small and require a manning increase to support this goal.

USARPAC receives a score of three for its satisfactory ability to support goal 2. USARPAC is increasing its organic conventional civil affairs capability, which will provide an increased ability to support this goal. However, at this time, this force change is in its infancy. The primary reason that USARPAC is better suited to support this goal is because of its experience in supporting this type of effort in operations in Iraq and Afghanistan over the past decade. This corporate knowledge of, in the field experience, affords a baseline across the USARPAC force. Although MARFORPAC, PACAF, and PACFLT forces supported Iraq and Afghanistan operations, Army personnel typically have more experience across their force in this arena.

Overall, the larger USPACOM functional component commands of PACFLT, PACAF and USARPAC are better suited to support the United States' strategic goal of "strengthening governance, rule of law and the fight against corruption"[171] This is primarily due these command's ability to use a larger pool of human resources. However, it is more likely that other United States' government organizations like the United States' Department of Justice are best suited to support this United States' strategic goal.[172] The highest score for any functional component command in terms of its ability

---

[171]Ibid.

[172]United States Department of Justice, http://www.justice.gov/ (accessed 8 October 2012).

to support this goal is a three. As such, this lends to periphery support by American armed forces of the United States' strategic goal. A graphic depiction of the results of this strategic goal comparison is at table 5.

Goal 3: Investing in People to Reduce Poverty

According to the United States' Department of State, this goal has three focus areas of education, health, and environment and disaster. Similar to the last two United States' strategic goals, the American armed services have minimal capabilities in supporting this goal. However, the capabilities that they can provide are critical to accomplishing this goal. According to the Department of State, the need to "reduce geographic disparities in health conditions," "increase household access to water and sanitation services," and an increase[d] effectiveness of disaster preparedness and relief programs" as major assistance approaches in this goal. [173] Table 4 shows the rubric for a score of one to four for each functional component based on its ability to improve the health sector; water and sanitation provision; and disaster preparedness.

MARFORPAC has a marginal ability to support this goal and receives a score of two from the rubric. Although Marines have provided disaster response to Pacific nations, that is not their primary function. The few medical personnel that MARFORPAC has are from the Navy and are not robust to the scale necessary to improve the Filipino health sector. Engineering capabilities in MARFOPAC are minimal as well and would not be able provide enough support water and sanitation provision.

---

[173]U.S. Mission to the Philippines, Appendix B.

73

PACFLT has a satisfactory ability to support goal 3, leading all of USPACOM's functional component commands. This score comes from increased ability in disaster preparedness support to the Filipinos. Because the Philippines are a coastal country with over 7,000 islands, maritime forces can support disaster preparedness of the Philippines better than ground forces.[174] PACFLT medical officers can support health concerns of the American State Department with focused training of Filipino doctors and administrators. PACFLT SEABEEs are able to help provision water and sanitation service. Because improving the health sector, water and sanitation provision and disaster preparedness are tertiary missions for PACFLT, they cannot receive a score of four in this category.

PACAF receives a score of two for its marginal ability to support this goal. PACAF forces are capable of providing support following a natural disaster and they can provide C-130 training to Filipino Air Force crewmembers prior to a natural disaster. However, training host nation aviation units is the most important part of the mission of SOCPAC aviation units.[175] One positive for PACAF forces in terms of its ability to support this goal is the capability to deploy to the Philippines from PACAF airfields without external support.

SOCPAC also receives a score of two in their ability to support the third goal. This score comes from SOCPAC's ability to deploy in small units to train Filipino forces to support their citizens. Furthermore, SOCPAC's ability to leverage civil affairs provides substantial connectivity to local medical and civil support leaders. Empowering

---

[174]U.S. Department of State.

[175]Special Operations Command, Pacific.

Filipino leadership to "invest in [its own] people to reduce poverty" provides sustainable progress towards this United States' strategic goal. [176]

USARPAC receives a score of two in their marginal ability to support this strategic goal. This score originates from the size of the USARPAC force. With a large force of American soldiers on the ground, supporting disaster preparedness across a large area is easier. Army medical units receive training to operate in austere environments and portions of the southern Philippines are often remote from major city centers. Doctors from USARPAC's 18th Medical Command can play an important role in supporting Filipino access to medical care. [177] Although USARPAC can support this goal because of its size, this factor can also be a detriment dropping their score from a three two a two. USARPAC will require other functional component commands or AFP to move its forces from island to island in the Philippines. A graphical depiction of the results of this strategic goal comparison is in table 5.

Goal 4: Promoting a Peaceful and Secure Philippines

From a military perspective, this goal is the easiest one for USPACOM functional component commands to support. Some of the focus areas for the United States' Department of State for this goal are "Philippine Defense Reform," counterterrorism efforts through training and equipping Philippine forces," and "modernization of the Armed Force of the Philippines based on U.S. Systems."[178] Although this is military

---

[176]U.S. Mission to the Philippines, Appendix B.

[177]US Army Pacific.

[178]U.S. Mission to the Philippines, Appendix B.

based goal, it does require a whole of government approach from the United States. Once again, organizations like the United States' Department of Justice can support Filipino law enforcement. [179] Table 4 shows the rubric for a score of one to four for each functional component based on its ability to provide counterterrorism support; mitigate terrorism and criminal activity in Mindanao; and strengthen AFP systems and personnel.

MARFORPAC, like PACFLT and PACAF, has a marginal ability to support this goal and receives a rubric score of two. MARFORPAC Marines can train Filipino Marines in amphibious operations necessary to come ashore on some of the lesser Filipino landmasses. Furthermore, MARFORPAC can train AFP on any new American systems they acquire that involve small unit ground combat operations. However, MARFORPAC lacks units specifically trained in counterterrorism activities.

Like MARFORPAC, PACFLT also lacks personnel trained in counterterrorism operations. PACFLT Sailors can train the Filipino Navy in sea-interdiction tactics necessary to impede terrorist transit between the Filipino islands of Sulu, Basilan, and Tawi Tawi. PACFLT's impact in this goal is marginal because it only affects the shorelines and territorial waters of the Philippines.

PACAF is not a counterterrorism force. As such, they have a marginal ability to support the fourth goal. PACAF Airmen can train the Filipino Air Force in operational tactics used for intelligence, surveillance and reconnaissance. Like the other USPACOM functional components, if the United States uses Security Assistance plan is to support

---

[179] United States Department of Justice.

76

"modernization of the [AFP] based on U.S. systems," each one of these functional components can provide tactics training and development.[180]

SOCPAC receives a score of four for its exceptional ability to support the fourth goal. This score comes from the fact that SOCPAC currently has forces deployed to the Philippines in support of this goal at this time and those forces have been in place for over ten years. SOCPAC's JSOTF-P is responsible for supporting Filipino forces in their efforts to combat insurgent terrorist organizations in the Southern Philippines.[181] These forces have supported the AFP in its combating terrorism activities for almost a decade and are on constant rotation from SOCPAC locations to the Philippines.

USARPAC has a satisfactory ability to support this goal and receive a score of three from the rubric. USARPAC's ability to put large forces on the ground to train AFP in counterterrorism activities is an important aspect to this goal. Understanding small unit tactics, troop leading procedures, and ground force non-commissioned officer skillsets are necessary in "mitigating criminal and terrorist activities" in the Philippines.[182] Although the abilities of USARPAC are important, USARPAC's deploying units sizes are detrimental to American – Filipino relationships. These large deployments of forces and large training venues are best suited for short duration training operations like Exercise Balikatan.[183] Supporting the Filipinos in a capacity building approach with an enduring presence is better suited for smaller footprint organizations. However, smaller

---

[180]U.S. Mission to the Philippines, Appendix B.

[181]Joint Special Operations Task Force–Philippines.

[182]U.S. Mission to the Philippines, Appendix B.

[183]Pike.

footprint organizations do not typically fill long and are not designed for long duration missions.

SOCPAC's corporate knowledge on the GRP's issues with terrorists in its country is a critical capability towards accomplishing the United States' strategic goal of "promoting a peaceful and secure Philippines." [184] These facts make SOCPAC the overall best USPACOM functional component command to support this final United States' strategic goal in the Philippines. Organizational history and the varying skills that the SOCPAC forces bring to the fight are lynchpin points to enable this goal.

Although each USPACOM functional component has merit in supporting the fourth goal, SOCPAC stands as the best-suited functional component command to support this goal. However, SOCPAC needs the support of the other functional components to accomplish its mission in the Philippines. SOCPAC requires PACFLT to provide counterterrorism interdiction support with the Filipino Navy in the vast waterways between the Philippines and Malaysia. SOCPAC requires MARFORPAC and USARPAC forces to support large troop training events like Balikatan. [185] Finally, SOCPAC requires PACFLT air assets to provide lift of vital support equipment around the Philippine Islands. SOCPAC is the force of choice, but SOCPAC cannot accomplish their support to the goal of "promoting a peaceful and secure Philippines" on its own.[186] A graphic depiction of the results of this strategic goal comparison is at table 5.

---

[184]U.S. Mission to the Philippines, Appendix B.

[185]Pike.

[186]U.S. Mission to the Philippines, Appendix B.

The GRP is working on peace pacts with different terrorist organizations in the Southern Philippines. On 7 October 2012, Filipino President Benigno Aquino III announced a preliminary peace deal with Moro Islamic Liberation Front (MILF).[187] The agreement with the MILF was planned for signature on 15 October 2012. The agreement creates an autonomous Muslim region in Mindanao, Philippines called "Bangsamoro." According to President Aquino, the GRP "would continue to exercise exclusive powers over defense and security, foreign and monetary policy in the new autonomous region, where Muslims would be assured of an 'equitable share of taxation, revenues, and the fruits of national patrimony... and equal protection of laws and access to impartial justice.'"[188] However, due to negotiation concerns in the MILF, the document was not signed on 15 October 2012, and is still in negotiation.

These types of agreements go a long way in helping the Filipinos achieve their National Security elements of socio-political stability, territorial integrity, economic solidarity, ecological balance, cultural cohesiveness, moral-spiritual consensus, peace, and harmony.[189] With these agreements in place, the counterterrorism goals of the United States' are realized. At that time, American military efforts in the Philippines can shift from counterterrorism to Filipino military capacity building and elements of Security Assistance.

---

[187]Eileen Ng, and Jim Gomez, "Philippines, Muslim rebels force peace pact," 7 October 2012, http://bigstory.ap.org/article/philippines-muslim-rebels-forge-peace-pact (accessed 8 October 2012).

[188]Ibid.

[189]Government of the Republic of the Philippines, *National Security Policy*, 4-6.

Table 6.　Department of State Goals Results

Functional Component Command	Department of State Goals (1=Fails, 2=Marginal, 3=Satisfactory, 4=Exceptional)				
	Accelerating Growth Through Increased Competitiveness	Strengthening Governance, Rule of Law, & the Fight Against Corruption	Investing in People to Reduce Poverty	Promoting a Peaceful and Secure Philippines	Goals Total
MARFORPAC	3	2	2	2	9
PACFLT	4	3	3	2	12
PACAF	3	3	2	2	10
SOCPAC	3	2	2	4	11
USARPAC	3	3	2	3	11

Source: Created by author.

Additional Factors

Along with each functional component's ability to support the goals, additional factors are considered. These factors are small ground unit capability, self-deploying capability and the ability to access culturally trained personnel. Each one of these factors facilitates the functional component's ability to support the goals in the Philippines.

Small ground units reflect a light American military presence and afford greater range of support to the AFP and GRP. PACFLT and PACAF receive a minimal score of zero for this identifier because across their commands their personnel do not deploy as small, minimally self-sufficient ground units. USARPAC receives a marginal score of one for this identifier because their forces are ground unit focused, but deploy as larger units for missions. MARFORPAC and SOCPAC receive a maximum score of two for this identifier because they have substantial small ground unit capability. MARFORPAC's scalability for operations is a standard deployment concept for the force. SOCPAC's special operations unit focus enables small ground units with tremendous support to achieve large results.

As shown in figure 2, the Philippines are a long way from American forces currently stationed in the Pacific. The ability to self-deploy allows the functional component to support the goals. MARFORPAC, SOCPAC, and USARPAC rely on other functional components or commercial contractors to deploy to the Philippines with personnel and equipment. Once inside the Philippines, these three functional components have marginal ability to move around the nation without additional support. This fact gives these three functional components a score of one in this additional identifier. PACAF and PACFLT are the only USPACOM functional components that have substantial self-deploying capability both getting to the Philippines and within the country's borders. As such, PACAF and PACFLT receive a score of two for this additional identifier.

MARFORPAC, PACFLT, and PACAF do not have culturally trained units at this time; therefore, they receive a score of zero for the access to culturally trained personnel additional identifier. Because USARPAC has the ability to use conventional civil affairs units from the Army and with the proposed regionally aligned units in the United States Army, USARPAC receives a score of one for this additional identifier. SOCPAC has the benefit of reaching across USSOCOM to access culturally trained personnel from multiple SOF units and receives a score of two for this identifier.

Table 7.   Additional Factors Results

Functional Component Command	Small Ground Unit Capability	Self-deploying Ability	Access to Culturally Trained Personnel	Factors Total
Additional Factors (0=no ability, 1=minimal, 2=substantial)				
MARFORPAC	2	1	0	3
PACFLT	0	2	0	2
PACAF	0	2	0	2
SOCPAC	2	1	2	5
USARPAC	1	1	1	3

Source: Created by author.

Combining the results from the goal comparison and the additional factors leads to a final USPACOM functional component conclusion.

Table 8.   Conclusion Table

Functional Component Command	Accelerating Growth Through Increased Competitive-ness	Strengthening Governance, Rule of Law, & the Fight Against Corruption	Investing in People to Reduce Poverty	Promoting a Peaceful and Secure Philippines	Goals Total	Small Ground Unit Capability	Self-deploying Ability	Access to Culturally Trained Personnel	Factors Total	Overall Total
Department of State Goals (1=Fails, 2=Marginal, 3=Satisfactory, 4=Exceptional)						**Additional Factors** (0=no ability, 1=minimal, 2=substantial)				
MARFOR PAC	3	2	2	2	9	2	1	0	3	**12**
PACFLT	4	3	3	2	12	0	2	0	2	**14**
PACAF	3	3	2	2	10	0	2	0	2	**12**
SOCPAC	3	2	2	4	11	2	1	2	5	**16**
USARPAC	3	3	2	3	11	1	1	1	3	**14**

Source: Created by author.

Recommendations

Based on the data from the conclusion table, SOCPAC, with a composite score of 16 is the best-suited force to support the United States' strategic goals in the Philippines. However, using all of USPACOM's functional components to support the goals is recommend because the requirements are too broad for one military force to be the sole solution provider to supporting American goals in the Philippines. There will be a shift in abilities across the forces as the American armed forces change in the Pacific and more forces become culturally aligned. In terms of size of the force versus capabilities, the USPACOM forces best aligned to support some of the American efforts in the Philippines are the forces under SOCPAC. Although SOCPAC's scores led to their forces being the best suited for three of the four goals, a SOF truth states, "Most Special Operations require non-SOF assistance."[190] This is evident by the need for SOCPAC forces support requirements of American conventional forces in the USPACOM AOR.

Areas for further study from this research center on expansion of United States and Filipino military interaction. If there is an expansion of American military under USPACOM, where should those forces reside? Should the conventional functional component commands have geographically aligned units focused on the Philippines like the ones that exist for Japan and Korea? Should USPACOM stand up an organization called United States Force – Philippines, as it has for Korea and Japan now? Should JSOTF-P transition to a conventional command or close as the GRP negotiates with the terrorist organizations in the Philippines?

---

[190]USASOC, "SOF Truths," http://www.soc.mil/USASOC%20Headquarters/SOF%20Truths.html (accessed 30 September 2012).

Linda Robinson, an adjunct senior fellow for U.S. National Security and Foreign Policy Council on Foreign Relations has some concerns on the relationship between SOF and conventional forces (CF). In her prepared statement on Special Operations Forces on 11 July 2012, she stated, "what is needed now is further progress on the institutional side of the house to provide more flexible combinations of SOF and CF that are tailored to the specific small-footprint missions that are likely to be the stock in trade of the future."[191]

For Filipinos and American strategic goals in the Philippines, that future is now. There is no one American military force under USPACOM best suited to support all four United States' strategic goals in this Philippines. As such, USPACOM planners should use caution in relying on one functional component command to carry the load in the Philippines. Having the right mix of American military forces that are able to support both Filipino and American strategic goals is key to assuring continued mutual support between the two nations. American and Filipino mutual support today will take a relationship forged in Manila Bay in 1898 with the words, "You may fire when you are ready, Gridley," into the future. [192]

.

---

[191]Linda Robinson, *Testimony on Special Operations—Hearing on the Future of Special Operations Forces* (Washington, DC: Council on Foreign Relations, 2012), 5.

[192]Hispanic Division.

BIBLIOGRAPHY

Books

Vandenbroucke, Lucien S. *Perilous Options: Special Operations as an Instrument of U.S. Foreign Policy*. New York: Oxford University Press, 1993.

Journals

JHU Gazette. "Historian Paul Kramer revisits the Philippine-American War." *The Johns Hopkins University Gazette*. 10 April 2006. http://www.jhu.edu/~gazette/2006/10apr06/10paul.html (accessed 7 May 2012).

Tan, Michelle. "Army now Reorganizing Geographically." *Army Times*, June 2012.

Government Documents

Congressional Research Service. *Pivot to the Pacific? The Obama Administration's "Rebalancing" Toward Asia*. Washington, DC: Congressional Research Service, 2012.

Department of Defense. *Capstone Concept for Joint Operations*. Washington, DC: Government Printing Office, 2009.

———. *National Defense Strategy*. Washington, DC: Government Printing Office, 2008.

———. *National Military Strategy*. Washington, DC: Government Printing Office, 2011.

———. *Quadrennial Defense Review Report*. Washington, DC: Government Printing Office, 2010.

Government of the Republic of the Philippines. *National Security Policy 2011-2016: Securing the Gains of Democracy*. Manila, Philippines: Government of the Republic of the Philippines, 2011.

Government of the United States of America, Government of the Republic of the Philippines. *Regarding the Treatment of United States Armed Forces Visiting the Philippines*. Manila, Philippines: United States Department of State, 1998.

Lum, Thomas. *The Republic of the Philippines and U.S. Interests*. Washington, DC: Congressional Research Service, 2012.

Olson, ADM Eric T. *United States Special Operations Command History*. Tampa, FL: USSOCOM, 2008.

Robinson, Linda. *Testimony on Special Operations.* Prepared statement before the House Committee on Armed Services Subcommittee on Emerging Threats and Capabilities, Washington, DC: Council on Foreign Relations, 2012.

Joint Chiefs of Staff. Joint Publication (JP) 1-02, *Department of Defense Dictionary of Military and Associated Terms.* Washington, DC: Government Printing Office, November 2010 (as amended through January 2012).

————. Joint Publication 3-05, *Special Operations.* Washington, DC: Government Printing Office, 2011.

————. *Joint Vision 2020.* Washington, DC: Government Printing Office, 2000.

United States Department of Defense and the Department of National Defense of the Republic of the Philippines. "Mutual Logistics Support Agreement." Washington, DC; Manila, Philippines, 2007.

United States Department of Justice. http://www.justice.gov/ (accessed 8 October 2012).

United States Department of State. http://www.state.gov/p/eap/ci/rp/ (accessed 13 May 2012).

————. "United States Department of State." 2012. http://www.state.gov/s/d/rm/index. htm#mission (accessed 7 August 2012).

————. Bureau of East Asian and Pacific Affairs. *Philippines.* 17 January 2012. http://www.state.gov/r/pa/ei/bgn/2794.htm#relations (accessed 21 September 2012).

————. *U.S. Department of State - Diplomacy in Action, Chapter 7-Legislative Requirements and Key Terms.* http://www.state.gov/j/ct/rls/crt/2007/103715.htm (accessed 21 September 2012).

U.S. Mission to the Philippines. *Country Assistance Strategy Philippines: 2009-2013.* Manila, Philippines: United States Department of State, 2009.

United States of America and Philippines. *Treaty of Manila.* Manila, Philippines: United Nations, 1946.

————. *Defense Status of Forces Agreement between the United States of America and the Philippines.* Manila, Philippines: United States Department of State, 1998.

————. *Manila Declaration.* Manila, Philippines: United States Department of State, 2011.

————. *Mutual Defense Treaty.* Manila: United States Department of State, 1951.

White House. *National Security Strategy.* Washington, DC: Government Printing Office, 2010, 20.

———. *Sustaining U.S. Global Leadership: Priorities for 21st Century Defense.* Washington, DC: Government Printing Office, January 2012.

Willard, ADM Robert F. "United States Pacific Command Strategic Guidance." Camp Smith Marine Corps Base, HI: USPACOM, 2011.

Internet Sources

13 AF. "13th Air Force." http://www.13af.pacaf.af.mil/ (accessed 6 August 2012).

25 ID. "The Mission of the 25th Infantry Division." http://www.25idl.army.mil/mission.html (accessed 6 August 2012).

5th BCD. "5th Battlefield Coordination Detachment." http://www.usarpac.army.mil/5thBCD/ (accessed 1 August 2012).

7th Fleet. "Commander, U.S. 7th Fleet." http://www.c7f.navy.mil/ (accessed 6 August 2012).

Ng, Eileen, and Jim Gomez. "Philippines, Muslim rebels force peace pact." *Associated Press.* 7 October 2012. http://bigstory.ap.org/article/philippines-muslim-rebels-forge-peace-pact (accessed 8 October 2012).

FAST. "Stevens Institute of Technology." *Filipino Association of Stevens Tech.* http://www.stevens.edu/fast/culture.html (accessed 25 September 2012).

Hispanic Division, Library of Congress. *The World of 1898: The Spanish-American War.* 22 June 2011. http://www.loc.gov/rr/hispanic/1898/chronphil.html (accessed 7 May 2012).

JSOTF-P PAO. "Joint Special Operations Task Force-Philippines." 24 February 2012. http://www.jsotf-p.blogspot.com/ (accessed 2 July 2012).

JTF-HD." Joint Task Force-Homeland Defense." http://www.usarpac.army.mil/docs/jtf-hd/ (accessed 1 August 2012).

Lewis, Martin W. "The Legacy of U.S. Military Bases in the Philippines," *GeoCurrents.* 21 October 2010. http://geocurrents.info/geopolitics/the-legacy-of-u-s-military-bases-in-the-philippines (accessed 12 May 2012).

McIlvaine, Rob. *U.S. Army.* 16 May 2012. www.army.mil/article/79919 (accessed 8 August 2012).

Miles, Donna. "U.S. Air Force." *Pacom weighs pre-positioning logistics for disaster response.* 31 July 2012. http://www.af.mil/news/story.asp?id=123312163 (accessed 21 September 2012).

Naval Air Forces. "Commander, Naval Air Forces." http://www.cnaf.navy.mil/ (accessed 6 August 2012).

Naval Surface Force, PACFLT. "Commander Naval Surface Force, U.S. Pacific Fleet." http://www.public.navy.mil/surfor/Pages/mission.aspx (accessed 6 August 2012).

PACAF. "Pacific Air Forces." http://www.pacaf.af.mil/ (accessed 6 August 2012).

PACFLT. "Commander, U.S. Pacific Fleet." http://www.cpf.navy.mil/ (accessed 6 August 2012).

Pike, John. "Exercise Balikatan: Shouldering the Load Together." *GlobalSecurity.org.* http://www.globalsecurity.org/military/ops/balikatan.htm (accessed 12 May 2012).

Rosenberg, Matt. "Mount Pinatubo Eruption," *About.com.* 11 November 2010. http://geography.about.com/od/globalproblemsandissues/a/pinatubo.htm (accessed 12 May 2012).

Special Operations Command, Pacific. "SOCPAC." http://www.socpac.socom.mil/ default.aspx (accessed 1 July 2012).

Submarine Force, PACFLT. "Submarine Force U.S. Pacific Fleet." http://www.csp. navy.mil/about_us.shtml (accessed 6 August 2012).

United States Coast Guard. "Pacific Area." http://www.uscg.mil/pacarea/ (accessed 6 August 2012).

United States Marine Corps. "U.S. Marine Corps Forces, Pacific." http://www.marforpac. marines.mil/ (accessed 6 August 2012).

USARPAC Webmaster. "Command Structure." http://www.army.mil/info/organization/ unitsandcommands/commandstructure/usarpac/ (accessed 1 August 2012).

USASOC. "United States Army Special Operations Command." http://www.soc.mil/ USASOC%20Headquarters/SOF%20Truths.html (accessed 30 September 2012).

USN NCD. "Welcome to the home of the SEABEES." http://www.seabee.navy.mil/ (accessed 6 August 2012).

USPACOM. "United States Pacific Command." http://www.pacom.mil/ (accessed 12 May 2012).

Whaley, Floyd. "Philippines Role May Expand as U.S. Adjusts Asia Strategy." *New York Times*, 29 April 2012. http://www.nytimes.com/2012/04/30/world/asia/ philippines-role-may-grow-as-us-adjusts-asia-strategy.html?pagewanted=all (accessed 21 September 2012).

White House. "The White House-President George W. Bush." *U.S.-Philippine Joint Statement on Defense Alliance.* November 2001. http://georgewbush-whitehouse.archives.gov/news/releases/2001/11/20011120-14.html (accessed 21 September 2012).

Other Sources

Clinton, Hillary Rodham. "Remarks With Secretary of Defense Leon Panetta, Philippines Foreign Secretary Albert del Rosario, and Philippines Defense Secretary Voltaire Gazmin After Their Meeting." Washington, DC, 30 April 2012.

Miller, Jr. Frank L. *Impact of Strategic Culture on U.S. Policies for East Asia.* Carlisle, PA: Strategic Studies Institute, 2003.

Simon, Sheldon. "The United States, Japan, and Australia: Security Linkages to Southeast Asia." The New Security Environment-Implications For American Security Conference, 4-5 April 2011, The National Defense University, Washington, DC.

Smith, Anthony L. "Reluctant Partner: Indonesia's Response to U.S. Security Policies." *Asia-Pacific Response to U.S. Security Policies* (March 2003): 88.

Supapo, Colonel Romulo C. *U.S.-Philippine Security Relations: Its Implication for the Global War on Terrorism.* Carlisle Barracks, PA: U.S. Army War College, 2004.

USARAK. *United States Army Alaska Pamphlet 600-2.* Joint Base Elmendorf-Richardson, AK: USARAK, 2010.

www.ingramcontent.com/pod-product-compliance
Lightning Source LLC
Chambersburg PA
CBHW081841280526
45789CB00007B/2535